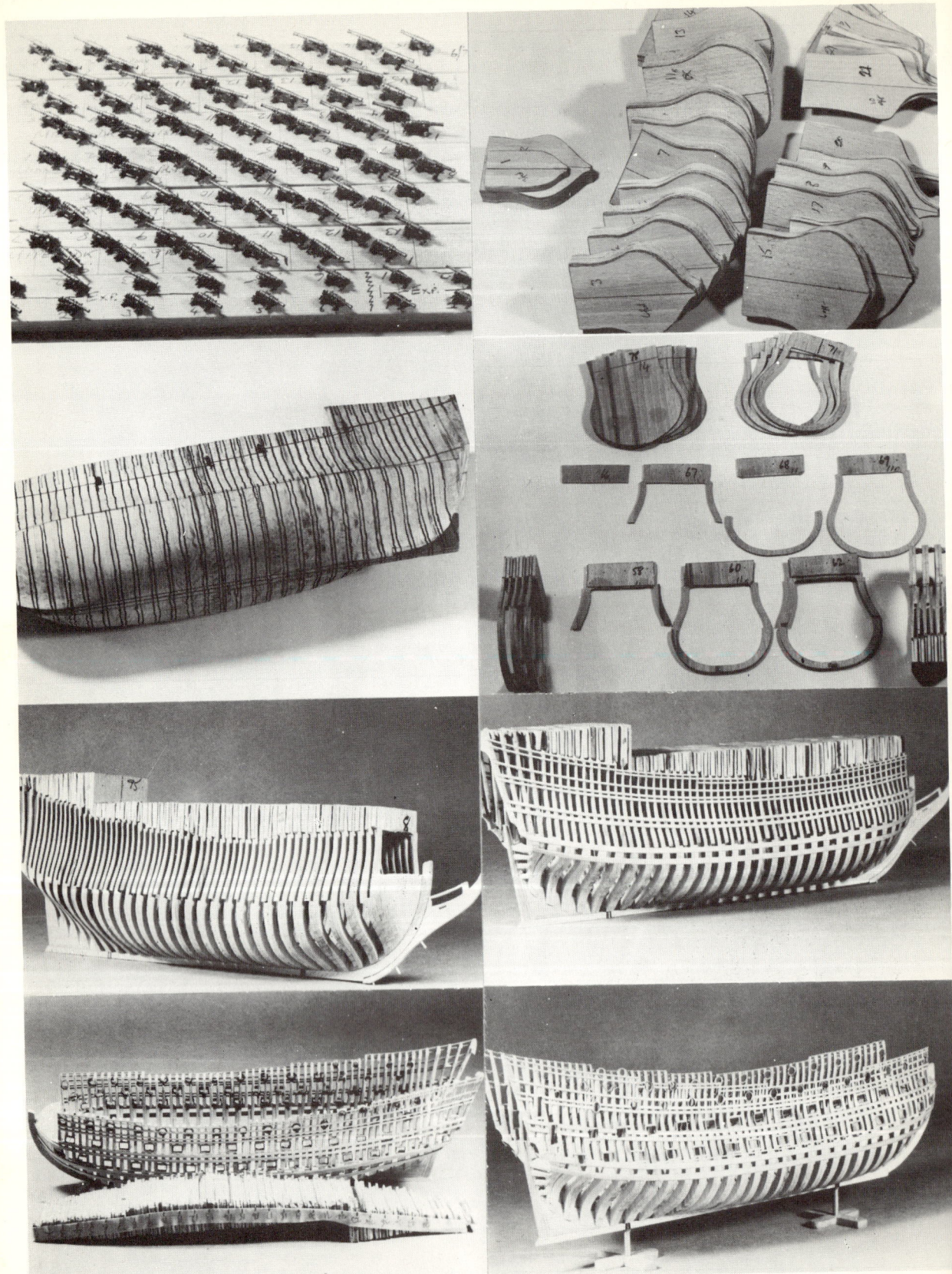

NUMBER 29
SEPTEMBER 1979

Managing Editor Robert Gardiner
Editor John Bowen, CEng, MRINA
Assistant Editor Roger Chesneau
Art Editor Ray Fishwick

model Shipwright

COMMENT

Once again the September issue is with us, and although the separate volume system has been dropped old habits die hard and I still look upon this as the start of another year of the journal. As ever, the past twelve months have been stimulating, have produced valuable contacts, and have opened up new areas of interest.

Your letters, whether they be seeking information - and what a wide field they embrace and how they reveal the handicaps under which so many labour - praiseworthy or critical, are always welcome and provide much useful material. Keep them coming, even though the replies to some may take longer than hoped. (Incidentally, it would be nice to hear, just now and again, from a few more than the present ten per cent who do take the trouble to reply, of the use to which the data supplied, often after lengthy research, has been put).

Some of the next year's plans were mentioned in the brochure, but I would like to take the opportunity to welcome our two new columnists. 'Plastics', in the widest context, are a comparatively new material (in comparison to wood and metal) for ship modelling and without doubt they have certain advantages, as has been shown in some previous articles. So with Roger Chesneau, one of the leading exponents of the craft of plastic modelling on the staff, what better than to give him space in each number to discuss the possible applications and techniques of this medium to certain areas of scale ship modelling. Over the years Brian King has contributed articles on a variety of topics, so we thought it was time to give him a regular spot in which to carry on the good work, particularly in reference to workshop practices and allied subjects.

Although the coming year will see new ideas and new contributors, plus some more from our regular authors, mutual help has always been one of our strong points. I am sure that with so many active modellers among our subscribers there must be much construction and research going on which would be of interest to others: how about putting pen to paper?

Finally, still on the subject of help, does anyone know of the whereabouts of plans of Thursday Island pearling luggers, and of a general arrangement and a lines plan for the tug HMS *Frisky* built in Aberdeen in 1918 and later to become the Canadian salvage tug *Foundation Franklin* (the shipbuilders have none)? If any readers have ideas for subjects for future articles in the 'Ships that Served', 'Miniature Merchantmen', and 'Classic Ships' series I would be pleased to hear about them. **John Bowen**

CONTENTS

© **1979 Conway Maritime Press Ltd**. All articles published in *Model Shipwright* are strictly copyright and may not be reproduced without the written consent of the publishers.
ISBN 0 85177 155 6
Published quarterly by Conway Maritime Press Ltd, 2 Nelson Road, Greenwich, London SE10 9JB.
Telephone 01-858 7211
Subscription Rates in UK £9 post paid for four issues published in September, December, March and June. Other rates on application.

Typesetting by Format Print Ltd, Erith, Kent.
Printed and Bound in the United Kingdom by Page Brothers (Norwich) Ltd.

Front Cover: HMS *Loyal London* of 1666 - another superb example of the craftsmanship of Donald McNarry. This model, to a scale of 1/16in = 1ft, is only 14¼in long.
Frontispiece: Trevor Manning's 3/8in = 1ft scale working model of the London to Leith Packet *Comet*, featured in this issue. (Photo: John Bowen).

HMS
LOYAL LONDON 1666

by Donald McNarry

The *London* of 1656 was accidentally blown up off the Nore Buoy in March 1665 with considerable loss of life. The euphoria of the Restoration of Charles II in 1660 still obtained in the Exchange and the City of London and a scheme was implemented to supply the King with enough money to build a replacement. (It would be nice to think of our present Stock Exchange passing round the hat for the latest thing in through-deck cruisers!).

The ship, this time called the *Loyal London*, was built by Commissioner Taylor at Deptford, and after three days' delay in getting her off the ways she was finally launched on 10 June 1666. Later that month Samuel Pepys records that every one of the great guns made for the *Loyal London* broke in pieces 'in the trial'.

She was eventually commanded by Sir Jeremy Smith, Admiral of the Blue and one of the Elder Brethren of Trinity House. A year later, during the great raid by the Dutch in the Medway she was burnt at her moorings with many other brave ships. There appear to be no known contemporary pictures of the *Loyal London*, not surprising for a vessel with such a short life.

An undistinguished warship and an unsuitable subject for a model – perhaps.

THE ORIGINAL MODEL
In the records of Trinity House, London is a minute of 1672 to the effect that 'Sir Jeremy Smith would speak to Mr Shish for a model'. Shish was Taylor's successor at Deptford, and the large model that for so many years stood in Trinity House was almost certainly the result of this minute. As the stern of the model bore, below the Royal Arms, the arms of Sir Jeremy combined with those of his second wife, a Miss Pockley, it is more than likely that this model represented the *Loyal London* – a dockyard model built after the original ship's destruction!

In the 1912 volume of the *Mariner's Mirror* Dr R C Anderson and Mr Gregory Robinson go into the matter in some detail and produce a good case for the correctness of this identification. Some thirty years later Dr Anderson had some second thoughts and perhaps by over-complicated theories seemed to doubt his original findings.

This Trinity House model was certainly unique. It was to a larger scale than other dockyard models, and much darker in appearance than usual. Most curious of all was the method of timbering, none of the double or single frames touching each other.

She was unplanked, but whilst there are other seventeenth century dockyard models also without planking all have their frames touching in certain areas so that solid belts of timber are formed along the length of the hull; however, on the *Loyal London* model the timbers are connected only by the keel, rails and wales outboard, and the keelson and deck clamps inboard. There were other quite inexplicable things on the model: the main channels were too short; the sheers of the hull timber ends followed a law of their own; both number eight gunports on the upper deck were rendered useless by the quarter-deck gangway steps; and all the lower gunports had mitred picture frames. There was much else besides.

Pepys reports that the *Loyal London* was reckoned to be one of the best vessels ever built for the Royal Navy and seems to imply that Taylor experimented somewhat. One cannot tell if these curiosities represent experimentation or whether the old, anonymous model builder didn't quite know what he was up to. After long study I fear the latter! However one cannot leave a description of this remarkable model just like that.

The Trinity House *Loyal London* must have had a really massive and magnificent appearance, more so than any other three-decker model. In contemplating her we have to accept the strange convention that, being an unplanked model, all the gilded carvings and decorations were applied direct to the timbers and framework; this gave the stern a truly fascinating appearance — entirely in frame, with gilt carvings superimposed. No planking, no panels, no windows, no doors. The two-tier quarter-galleries were done in the same way, their complicated shapes being even more pleasurable to look at.

The original model was destroyed by fire in a German air raid on 29 December 1940. It is now replaced by a modern version made by the late Robert Spence and the marine artist Leslie Wilcox.

THE PRESENT MODEL

I first came across the *Loyal London* model soon after the war when I bought a second-hand copy of Culver's *Contemporary Scale Models of Vessels of the 17th Century* (1926) and subsequently obtained eight magnificent 12in x 9in *Country Life* photographs of the original model, probably taken just after the first war. The original photographer is unknown but he had an eye for the right angle when photographing such things and two of the pictures especially, the starboard bow/broadside view and the port quarter/stern view, are to me quite breathtaking and must surely be two of the best photos of a ship model ever taken.

As long ago as the early 1950s it

was in my mind that I should do a 16in = 1ft dockyard model of the *Loyal London*, but the difficulty of producing this fashion of timbering at so small a scale seemed insurmountable and I realised that if it could be done in miniature it would be the most advanced and difficult ship model building it was possible to undertake. There was also the usual problem of there being no plans. However one of the photos was a good, even, broadside view with apparently little distortion, — in theory at least it should give me reasonably accurate measurements of all heights from keel to rail and all lengths from bow to stern.

So, combining this with Anderson's dimensions in the *Lists of Men of War, 1650–1700,* sparse enough at 127ft x 41ft 9½in and 1134 tons, I produced, at odd moments over a period of years, several elevation drawings, the last of which seemed about as good as I would get and showed all the timbering, deck levels, ports, etc.

With eight photos clearly showing the original model at various angles the only proper way to get the body plan sections was by geometrical photo analysis. I have read Underhill's explanation of the process and have had it laboriously explained to me from other sources but I am afraid the whole concept is quite beyond me — I don't even begin to understand it.

Another method of producing ship's lines, perhaps the best method when there is the minimum of information, is the system I call the Deane/Abell/Freeston process described in Deane's *Doctrine of Naval Architecture, 1670,* reproduced by Westcott Abell in *The Shipwright's Trade* in 1948 and subsequently by Ewart C Freeston in Mr W O B Majer's long-lost and lamented *Sheet Anchor* and again in the earlier pages of this journal. I don't find this easy either but it is one of the original methods and should be persevered with. The whole business of plans for models of seventeenth century vessels is very difficult indeed. Some original models have had their lines taken off and published and sometimes one can use these for similar vessels,

making modifications to the dimensions of the subject as one proceeds. Invariably, though, no one knows the true form of the original ship's hull, and in the present case of course we don't even know the true form of the Trinity House model and can only hope to get something near it.

Once the elevations and cross sections were done it was no great difficulty with the aid of these and the photos to get out the five deck plans. If one has a good broadside view of a ship it is remarkable how accurately this can be made to dictate the position of most of the items on a deck plan. At this stage I had many other models to make so I put all the work away for a long period without looking at it, a famous idea for seeing the errors on next inspection.

But I did not stop thinking about the problem of producing a hull of disconnected timbers. As will be seen by some of the photographs the eventual idea was to cut all the frames with an extended piece above bulwark level and to firmly glue these together on reassembly into a solid laminate — a somehow dominating and ominous collection of timber which came to be known by me as the 'wodge'.

Small spacing pieces were temporarily glued between the lower timber ends just above the keel level to keep all these in position. This method wastes timber but I still can't think of a better way to solve the problem, indeed I now use something of a similar arrangement on ordinary dockyard models. The disadvantage is of course that one has to work for weeks and weeks before carefully sawing off the wodge to discover only then if the plan view of the bulwark tops is even and symmetrical. I don't know what one does if it is not.

Once this is off and the keel, keelson, wales etc are on, a remarkably strong and taut construction results. From this point onwards it is just ordinary dockyard model work of building up one deck after another, fitting the gun carriages and checking the mast alignments. With armed dockyard models I make the complete

set of guns first before starting the model; the fitting of the carriages and the removal and re-fitting of the barrels is so intimately connected with the interior building up of each deck that it is the only possible way of doing it.

The framework for the stern and quarter-galleries was one of the most interesting parts of the construction. In recent years I have evolved a method of making various very thin plys from 18in x 1¾in yellow cedar plane shavings, ideal material for taking liberties with in such involved shapes as the *Loyal London* quarter-galleries.

In describing the original model I should have mentioned that the rigging shown in the photographs was obviously not the original but latter-day anachria and could be ignored. As usual, Anderson's two books produced the spars and rigging on the present model. Working out all the sizes and proportions used to be a rather boring and long-winded process of lots of simple arithmetic, now made very much easier and quicker with a pocket calculator.

FINISHING TOUCHES

The carved and gilded stands supporting the model are of three dolphins, the fore and aft ones having tridents in their mouths; the stands also incorporate the shield from the arms of the City of London St George's Cross and the sword of St Paul. The case is of natural, half-filled and semi-limed English oak with a satin finish. A matching shelf with two hanging knees supports the case on the wall with the added security of long screws through to the case. These have

Below and opposite: sheer perfection in detail is the only way to describe these various views of the model and of the stands. Remember, when looking at these photographs, that the hull is only about 8in long.
All photographs by the Author.

ornamental bosses showing the full arms of London on the face and the enscrolled motto *Domine Dirige Nos* around the side, enamelled in full colour.

The nice, comfortable pages of *Model Shipwright* are not the place to discuss the unacceptable and harsh powers of the Customs & Excise for the collection of VAT. Suffice it to say that if a professional ship model builder wishes to remain free of this he is very limited in his professional output. Consequently models of major vessels like the *Loyal London* cannot be offered for sale. Unpleasant though all this is I can record an amusing tail-piece resulting from it.

Not long ago we had a visit from an American client who came over specially to collect another dockyard model of mine. During the course of conversation, repeated, enthusiastic and I must say appreciated efforts were made to buy the *Loyal London* as well. I mentioned the sales tax problem (a desperate thing indeed to attempt to explain the stultification of our bureaucracy to a free American!) and after some thought he offered me a bar of gold, he having a perfectly proper professional facility for obtaining such things.

The exotic illegality of this appealed very greatly but we do not really want to sell the model and my wife could not see herself taking the ingot to the grocers every week and shaving off a thin slice to pay the bill. We could have used it for a door stop though — it would have been perfectly safe since no one would have believed it genuine.

However, the *Loyal London* remains on the sitting room wall.

THE 'COOKE' MUD DREDGER

by Dr G Santi-Mazzini

When I came into possession of a copy of E W Cooke's book *Shipping and Craft* (published in 1829) I was fascinated more by the unsightly vessels — as I would call them — than by the better looking ones, and in particular by the mud dredger shown in Plate 17. Another point which attracted me to this particular vessel was that it illustrated the early application of power, in this case steam, to an onerous task, namely dredging, and this was at that time a very important step in the development of harbour maintenance. Furthermore, I feel that modelmakers and those interested in maritime affairs tend all too often to neglect one of the most important branches of marine technology, — the service craft found in rivers, docks and harbours.

For these reasons I decided to build a model of this most intriguing vessel. As a start I wrote to the National Maritime Museum at Greenwich to find out if they had any plans of this type of craft. They had none of this actual vessel but they were able to supply two draughts of dredgers of the same period, though these were very different in appearance. Even so they were quite useful as they gave me a good idea of the general layout of the hull and machinery, although that of the steam engine appeared to me to lack detail of some of the equipment. Thus my principal source of information was the Cooke engraving. Although this is remarkable for its clarity and detail, I must confess that I was unable to find an explanation for all of the

details shown; I would be glad of any help in this direction which readers can offer. Although I have answered the following questions, as will be seen shortly in this article, nevertheless I would like to have readers opinions on these points:
1 What was the form of the hull, and what were its dimensions?
2 What kind of steam engine was used?
3 How was the driving transmission arranged?
4 How was the bucket chain frame adjusted for various dredging depths?
5 How was the dredger moved?

THE HULL AND SUPERSTRUCTURE

The NMM draught showed a vessel whose bow and stern were to me too sharp in comparison to the engraving, so I decided that a more acceptable shape would be that of the *prame* (Falconer: a sort of lighter, formerly used in the ports of the Baltic Sea and in Holland for loading and unloading ships). There was no doubt in my mind that the bottom would be quite flat. So far as size was concerned, I based my drawing on the height of a seaman and on the angle made by the two large supports for the bucket frame. I admit that this is not a scientific method, but being without any other data I was obliged to work in this way; in spite of it, the outcome seems to me to be acceptable. The dimensions which I worked out in this way were, at a scale of 1/50 - length overall 600 mm, beam 212mm, draught 40mm,

corresponding to 30m x 10.6m x 2m (98.4ft x 34.7ft x 6.6ft).

The superstructure was not hard to interpret, and is quite modern in appearance - four angled main columns carry two horizontal beams, which in turn support a shaft carrying two gear wheels. The after ends of these beams are connected to what I have called the engine structure, which in turn is made up of eight vertical columns, two horizontal beams, and a number of cross members. Extending above this whole structure is a lighter one which carries the bucket frame. As this bucket frame passes through the hull at the fore end, there must be some form of opening in the hull for it. The deck layout, from what can be seen in the engraving, appears to be as follows: the fore end is given over to a galley (j), to a chain locker, and possibly to some sort of simple accommodation. The space below the engine structure contains the engine and any associated items, with immediately aft of this a square space for the boiler; finally at the after end there is a coal bunker on the port side and possibly some kind of water supply tank on the starboard side.

MACHINERY

There were many similarities between the NMM plan and the Cooke engraving. However the cylinder is not visible, and the position of the steam pipe (a) has been estimated. I think the Cooke dredger probably had a vertical engine with a beam lever, the fulcrum of which was on the port

Above: the engraving from E W Cooke of the English mud dredger.

cross member, with the connecting rod on its starboard side and any other auxiliary equipment connected to the beam between the fulcrum and connecting rod, ie, air pump and condenser, and water pump. A steam valve system was shown in outline only on the NMM plan, so again I had to do some guesswork here, and decided that the only possible position for its eccentric sheave and rod was opposite the flywheel, at the other end of the crankshaft. Another detail not visible on the engraving was any form of governor gear; it must have been somewhere. Considering the two items (a) and (b), the steam pipe and the exhaust valve, it is evident from the engraving that they are connected by a system of levers, and that the lever (c) must have been moved by a governor to open or shut the

throttle valve in the steam pipe and at the same time operate the exhaust valve. The latter is an unusual type to find on this kind of marine engine, being more usual on the early locomotives.

The boiler must have been of a very simple type; there were no tubes, just a combustion chamber under a water tank. Had it not been for the details on the NMM plan I would never have accepted such an arrangement. This boiler must have had a water gauge; in my model I made a mistake because I provided it with a glass tube, which I discovered later was only fitted in the latter half of the 19th century. At this period the gauge consisted of three cocks, the uppermost for an excessive water level, the middle for the correct level, and the lowest one for insufficient water.

The three pumps had the following functions: the first, near the piston rod created a vacuum in the condenser while a cold water jet changed the state of the steam; the second drew the warm water

from the condenser and returned it to the boiler; and the third drew in salt water for cooling the whole apparatus, and this was then discharged overboard through a pipe on the starboard side. I have omitted any reversing gear, as I was not sure of its kind or even if any such thing was fitted, and finally I have not been able to make out the function of the detail marked (i) on the top of the engine structure.

THE TRANSMISSION
In the engraving the drive shaft is shown wholly covered, but in the NMM plan it shows it in the open. The after end is attached to the crankshaft by some sort of coupling, and the forward end connects to a second shaft through bevel gears; it is supported by two bearings fitted on the inside cross members. This second shaft runs up the side of the bucket frame to connect by means of a crown wheel and pinion to a horizontal transverse shaft which carries the drive for the bucket chain.

Below: this gives a good idea of the construction of the superstructure; note the mud chute, tarpaulin by the bucket well, and 'atmosphere' on the after deck.
Opposite: the completed model.

THE BUCKET CHAIN

At this point in my interpretation of the engraving I faced the question of the function of the large hand-wheel (k), the large gear wheel (x) and the handwheel (e). As this system of dredging cannot alter the angle of the bucket frame to suit varying conditions, it was necessary to lift or lower the frame to suit the depth of water. This was indicated on the NMM plan, where such movement was accomplished by means of a third bevel wheel. But in the engraving there is a difference: the gearwheel (x) cannot do anything but move the bucket frame, but how it does so is not shown. I had already observed that there was nothing casual about anything depicted on Cooke's engravings, so the two points (f) and (g) had to have some meaning. I took them to be the outboard ends of two shafts each of which was operated by a pinion engaging with the large gearwheel (x). The after shaft (f), I suggest, carried a barrel on which was wound a cable, the free end of which was led to and

wound on a second barrel on a shaft supported by a pair of bearings attached to the after face of the sloping supports for the bucket frame. This latter shaft was driven from the main shaft by means of a worm wheel and pinion, which was engaged when it became necessary to move the bucket frame. This was accomplished by means of a clutch operated by the small handwheel (e). The free end of the cable mentioned above, after being wound on the barrel, had a counterweight attached to it to act as a simple tensioning device. The forward shaft (g) was similar to (f) but its cable was fixed to the lower part of the bucket frame, so that the sequence of operations was as follows: the clutch was engaged by operating the handwheel (e), whereupon the cable was wound on to the barrel on this shaft from the barrel on shaft (f), this action causing shaft (f) to rotate and so drive the large gearwheel (x) by means of the pinion. The rotation of (x) in turn operated shaft (g) through its pinion, and this in turn wound cable on to its drum and so elevated (or lowered) the bucket frame. If the engine was not fitted with any form of mechanical reversing gear, the only way of altering the direction of rotation would have been by moving the flywheel over by hand once the steam supply had been cut off by means of the valve (b).

The bucket chain was not composed of a constant number of units. It ran between two points, a fixed one at the top and a

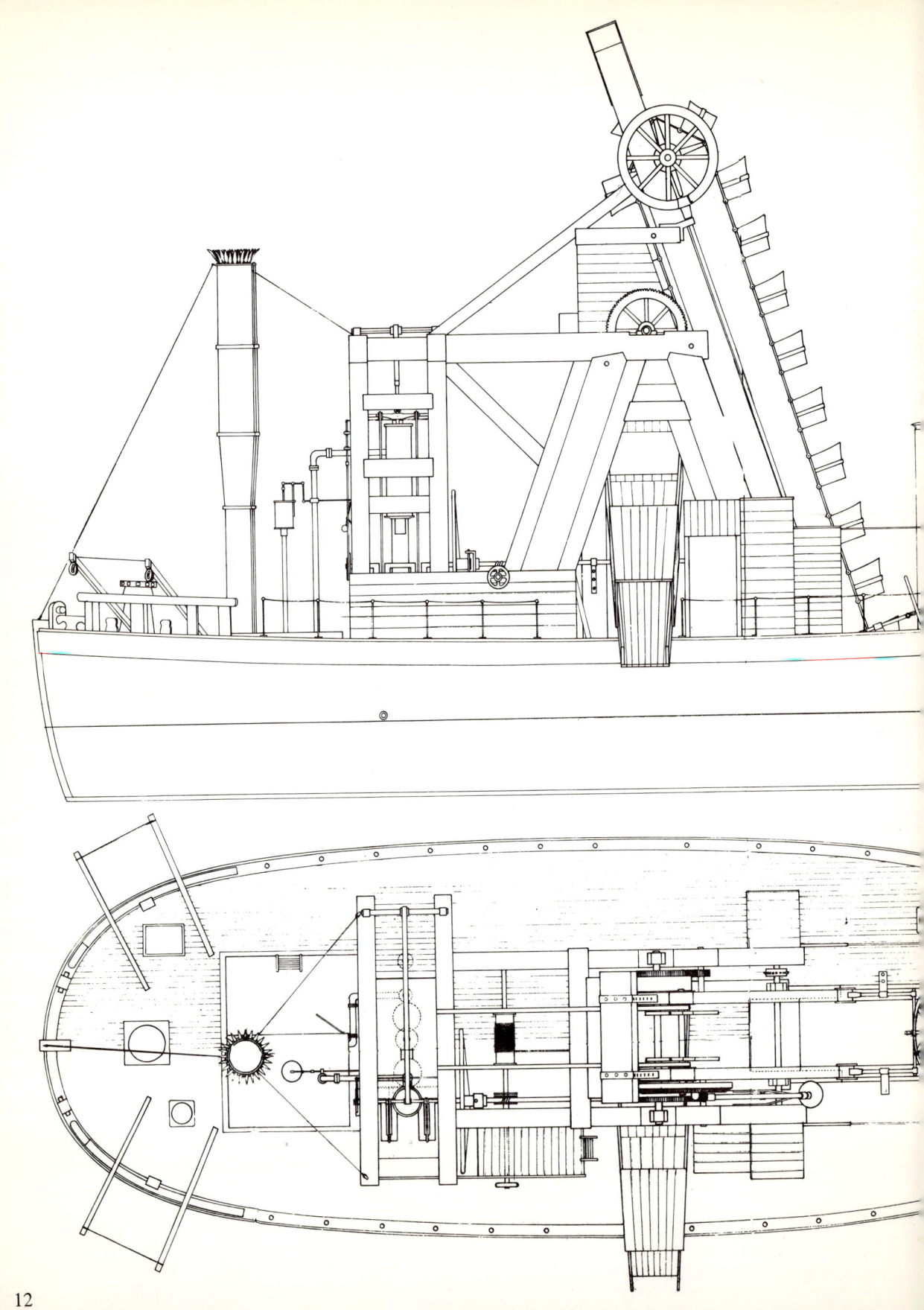

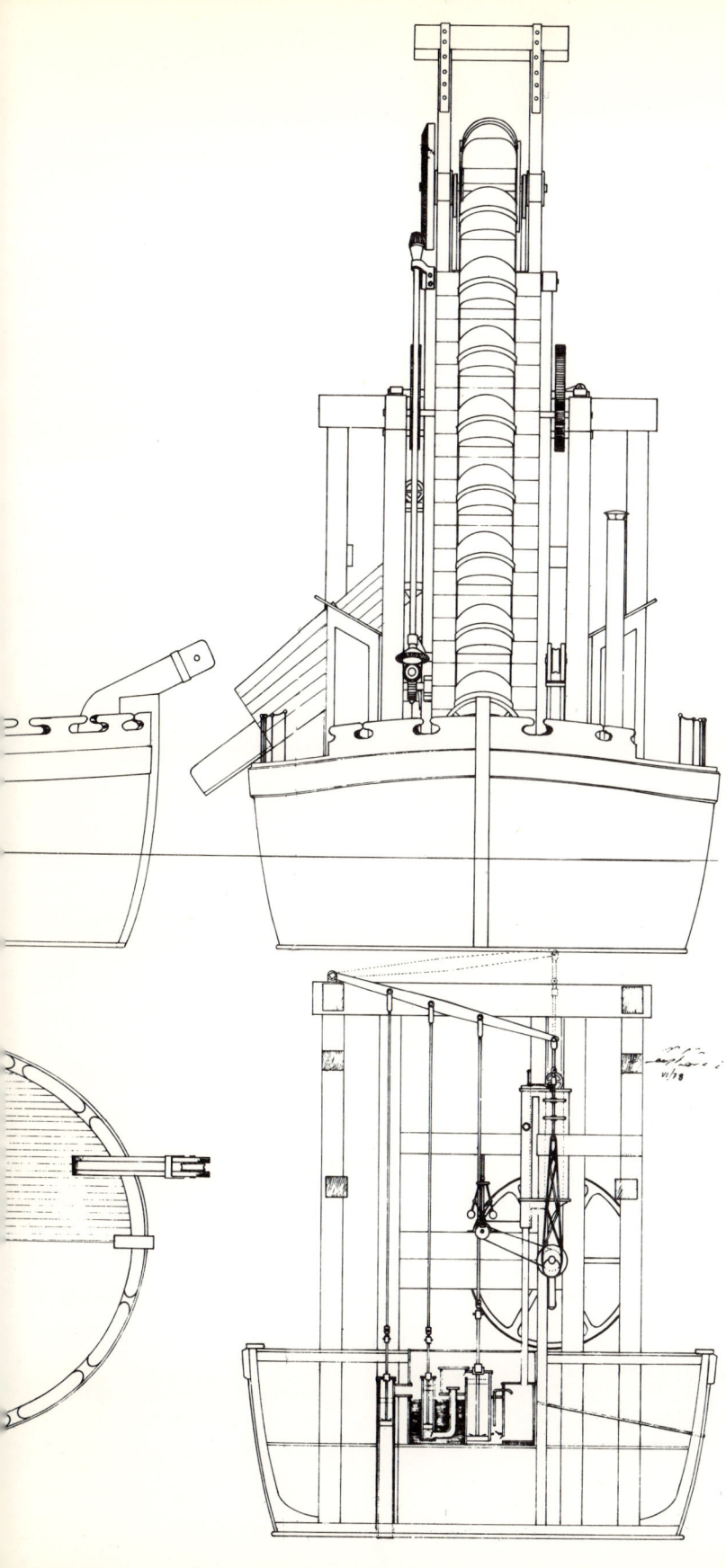

movable one at the bottom of the frame. The length of the chain was dependent on the depth to be dredged, and the number of buckets on the chain was altered to suit. With this in mind I reflected for some time on the use of the large handwheel (k), which was set at an angle to the horizontal and appeared to be at right angles to the bucket frame. This led me to think that it operated some form of brake mechanism on the bucket frame, which would obviously have to be well secured when dredging. So I fixed the handwheel on to a shaft the fore end of which was pivoted on an angled bracket and the other end threaded through the centre of a horizontal shaft the ends of which operated the braking mechanism. The upper fixed point for the bucket chain was necessary because the shaft carrying the large crown wheel (y) was supported by two beams with two rollers upon which the bucket frame ran; this point was thus independent of the motion of the bucket sliding frame.

In operation, when the buckets reached the top and turned, the contents were discharged into the square opening formed by the short tie members joining the upper ends of the large inner supports. On the engraving is a detail (h) which may be some sort of internal screen to stop the mud going out. The mud then drops down on to the sloping trough placed under and between the large sloping supports and thence down into the mud barge alongside. I think the erections (v) and (w) on the side of the structure might be for cleaning tools, and those on the port side companionways.

PROPULSION

Then there is the matter of how the dredger was moved, since it had neither paddles or screw. The engraving shows a cable (p) and a chain (o) at the bow, the cable being made fast to a mooring (q) and the chain presumably to an anchor. Thus the dredger moves forward by heaving on the chain by means of a windlass. The NMM plan showed a rudder but I do not

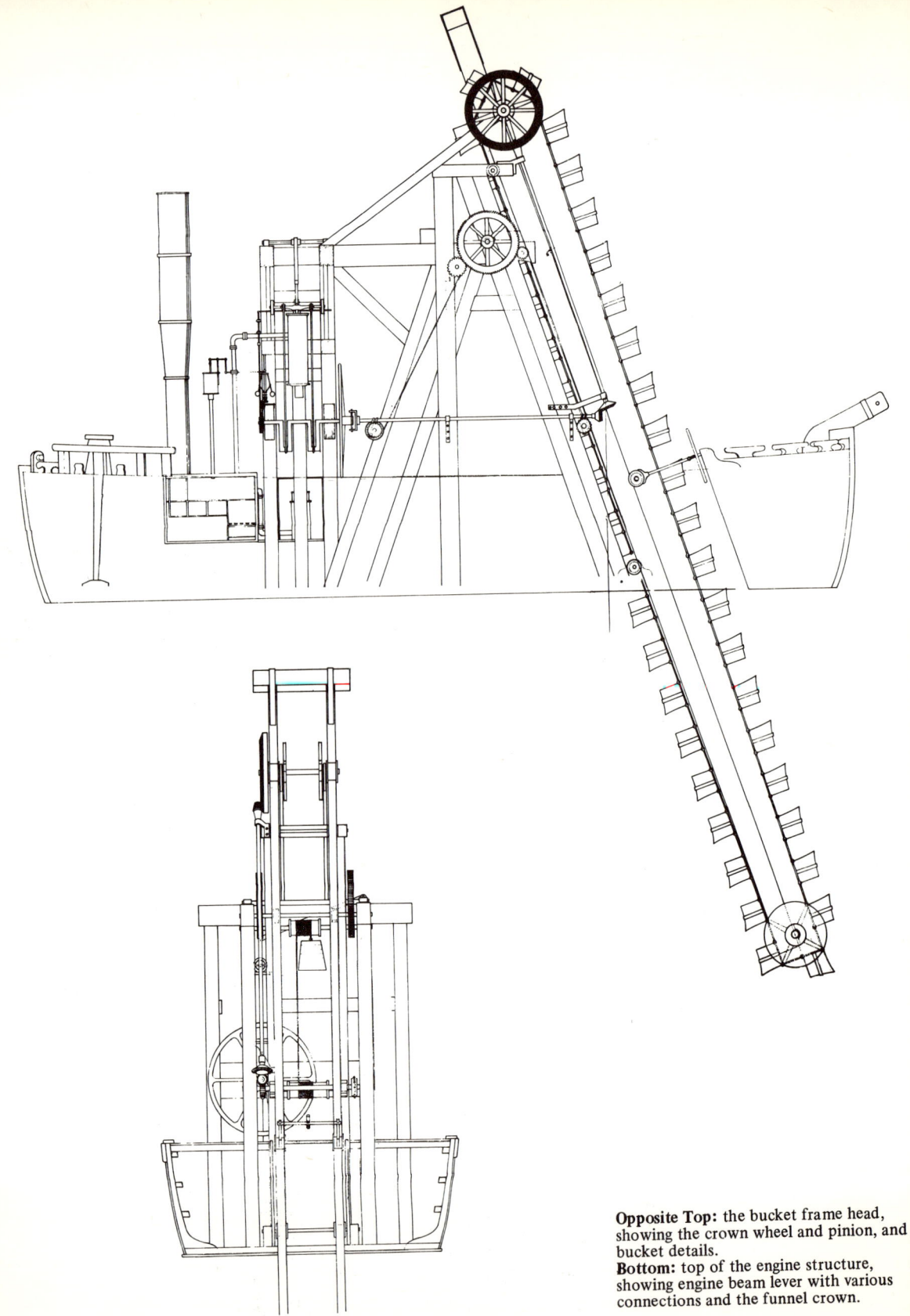

Opposite Top: the bucket frame head, showing the crown wheel and pinion, and bucket details.
Bottom: top of the engine structure, showing engine beam lever with various connections and the funnel crown.

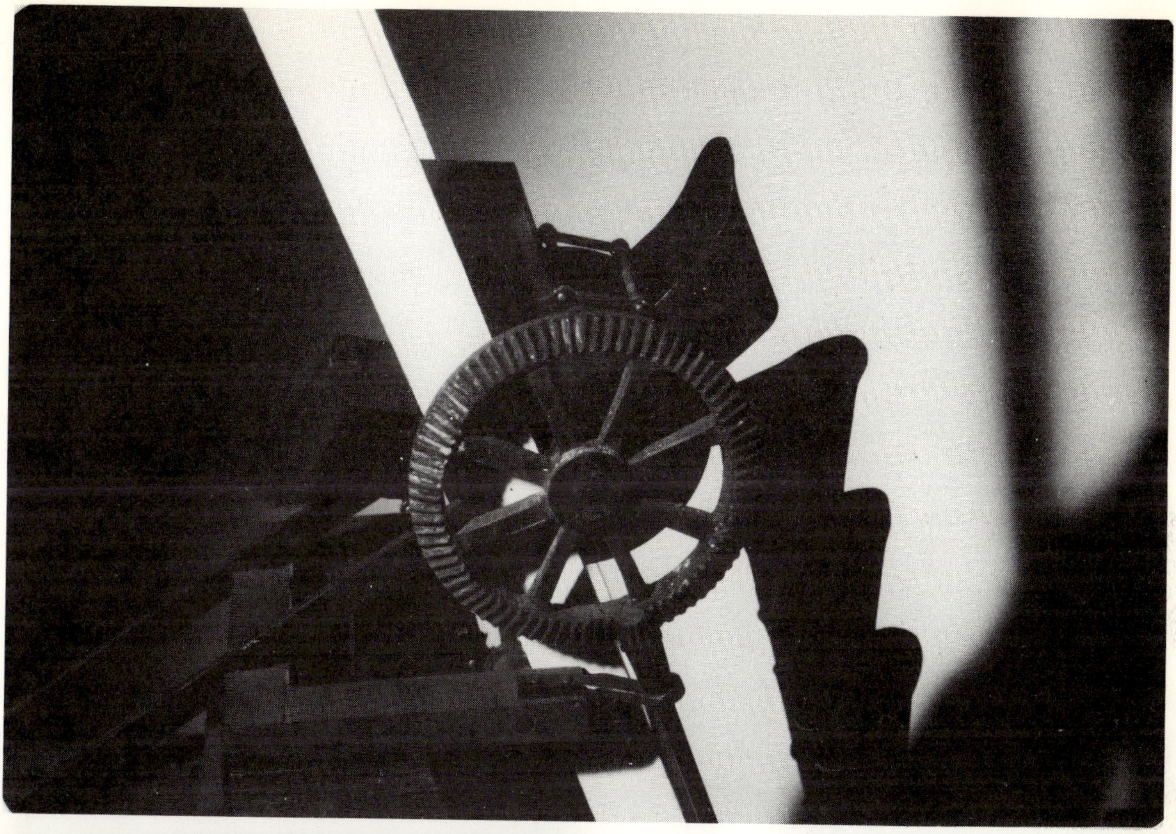

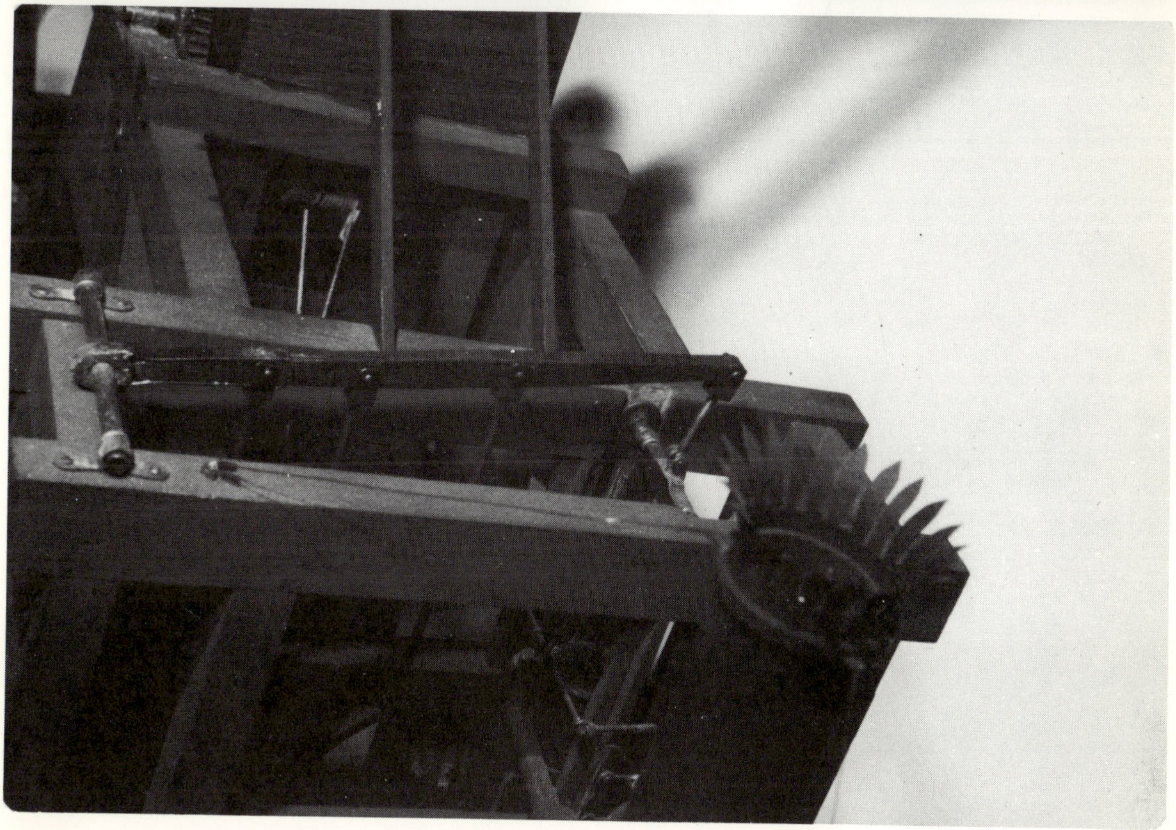

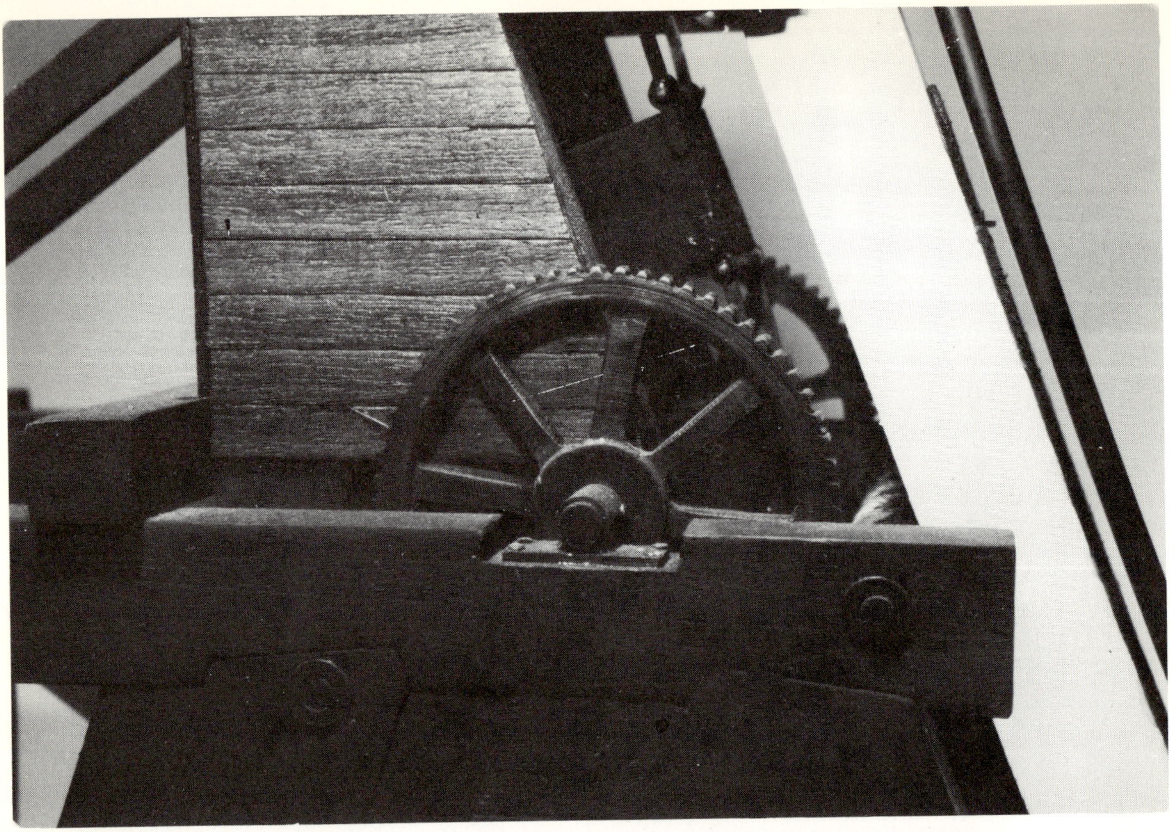

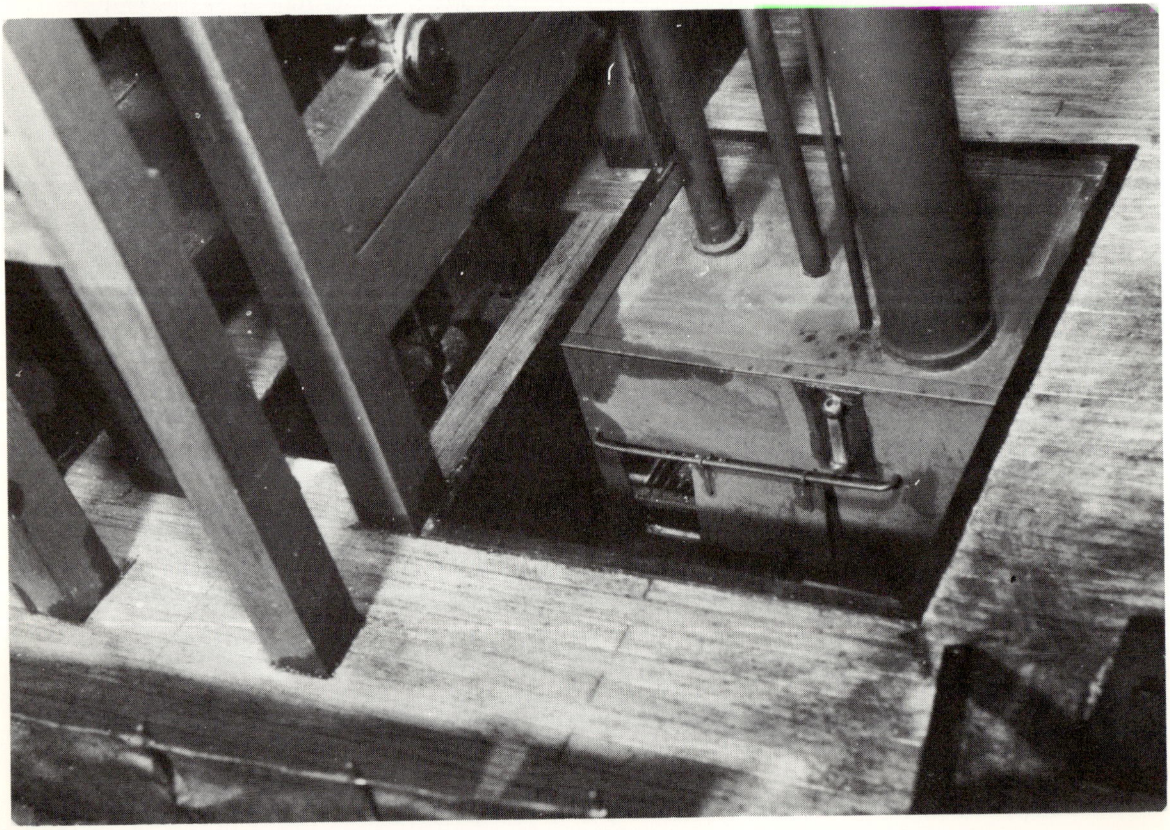

Opposite Top: top of main superstructure frame, showing the large gearwheel (x) and the two transverse shafts (f) and (g).
Opposite Bottom: looking down on the top of the boiler, and showing the bottom of the supports forming the engine structure.
Right: the handwheel and brake mechanism, and more details of the construction of the bucket chain.

think that this vessel had one, particularly as in the engraving there is a barge lying athwart the stern. In any case it would have moved only along fixed lines.

The only other details in the engraving for which I have not been able to determine the use are the two pairs of davits at the after end (m) and (n). Were they for carrying a workboat, or were they used for loading coal and stores?

BUILDING THE MODEL

I will not dwell on the way I made the hull, as any suitable method can be used; the real interest in the model lay in the construction of the upperworks and the machinery. So far as the engine is concerned it could be made to work, in which case the book *Model Stationary and Marine Steam Engines* by K N Harris (Argus Books) will be found to be useful. I did not make mine to work. Whichever is done, a lathe is essential, and for producing the gears some form of milling machine is necessary. Unfortunately I did not have such an attachment for my Unimat lathe, so had to make up. I will not go into all the details of its contruction here, as it really needs a separate article. However it was based on the Dremel Moto-drill Press No 210 to which I attached a simple double slide made of brass, and a 360° goniometer or dividing head. The teeth were cut with a 1mm mill which I happened to have. Though his set-up appeared to be too

rough for accurate work, the results were nevertheless satisfying. Going back to the engine for a moment, it could be built as shown, but the boiler/furnace area would have to be suitably lagged, and the boiler itself could not be of the original shape. In my opinion, it would be better to use an electric motor with suitable low gear ratio driving directly on to the crankshaft; this would have two advantages — less trouble and a chance to incorporate radio control.

As with the hull, the construction of the superstructure was quite simple, as can be seen from the plans which accompany this article, and the same applied to the deck fittings, though there are one or two points which may

be of interest and use in other models. The buckets would have been quite simple to build had they been of a 'half bell' shape, when it would have been a matter of turning them and then cutting in half. However, they were flat bottomed with rounded corners on the leading edge. I made them of thin copper sheet cut to the shapes shown in the diagram. To produce the fore wall I made a pair of wood moulds to the finished shape, placed the flat, shaped, copper sheet between them and squeezed them together. Though rudimentary this method worked, and all that remained was to solder the three pieces together.

I cut the funnel crown from brass sheet, the method being

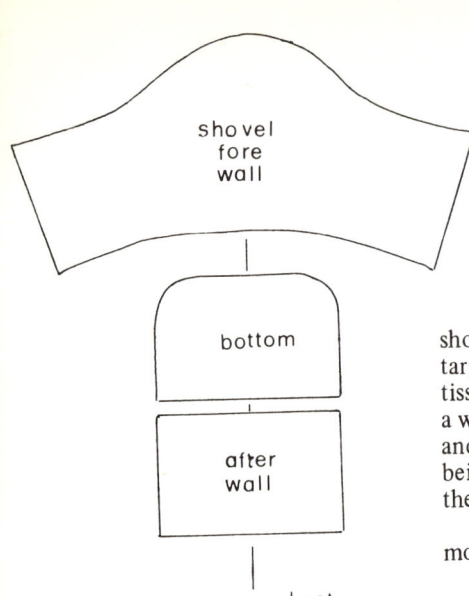

shovel
fore
wall

bottom

after
wall

copper sheet
patterns

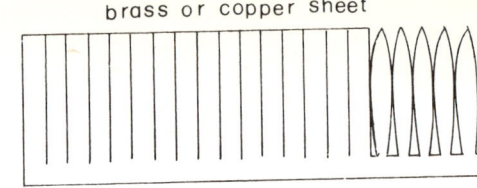

brass or copper sheet

operating for chimney crown
making

shown in the diagram. The tarpaulins I made from very thin tissue paper, which I soaked in a watery solution of indian ink and glue, the result when dry being a hard thin sheet just like the tarpaulin.

Finally I decided to give the model some atmosphere, for these vessels were never clean, especially in the furnace and coaling areas. For this I used vegetable coal dust (normally for laboratory use; charcoal?) which is very fine, and when moistened becomes quite like the dark mud.

BIBLIOGRAPHY
Cooke, E W : *Shipping and Craft* (London, 1829)
Hardy, A C : *Modern Marine Engineering* (London, 1948)
International Marine Engineering (1913)
Massero, F : *Disegno di Macchine* (Milan, 1953)
Uccelli, A : *Storia della Tecnica* (Milan, 1947)

Below: the engine 'flywheel' showing the clutch connection to the main drive shaft, and the worm and pinion gearing connecting the bottom cross shaft carrying the cable drum for operating the hoisting gear of the bucket frame.
All photographs by Italo Turci.

Brian King's Column

Having written a fair amount about a variety of matters for *Model Shipwright* I think the editor felt he ought to tidy up my meanderings into a column probably headed by the caption 'Not all ideas expressed in this section are necessarily those of the editor'. Seriously, it will give me a chance to range across the spectrum of *Model Shipwright* interests and to write about either one topic, as in this issue, or about several, perhaps quite unlinked subjects, at other times. Mostly the accent will be on 'production problems', ie workshop-based, although occasionally the area covered may extend beyond the boundries of the workbench. It may well be that you have ideas as to what should be said, and any suggestions would be most welcome, not that I can claim to be an expert on anything. If it is possible then I will write about suggested items. Further, newcomers to the model shipwright scene with problems might like to write to me. Perhaps a problem could be dealt with privately, and if of general interest, published at a later date. Obviously a question and answer page in a three-monthly journal is impracticable; the period between writing and publishing may be as long as 12 months. You can reach me care of *'Shipwright'* of course.

Incidentally I am still being asked if prints of my version of Dr Rose's saw are still available (*Model Shipwright* No 20). They are, price £3.50 — post free, of course.

AIRBRUSHES

Most model makers with any degree of practical ability make at least a fair job of the constructional side of a model. The real snag, the 'Achilles heel' of many models, lies in the finishing. However good the model is in the 'white' the final finishing is where the crunch comes — whether the excellence found in the making can be matched with the excellence of the finish. Only too often it cannot, and the finish lets the model down. Much can be said and has been said about finishing. I intend only to concentrate on one aspect and that is getting the paint, lacquer, etc on to the model.

There are of course those of us who use brushes camel, sable or nylon and very fine paint jobs can be turned out provided brush, paint and conditions are correct. There is no denying this, but I venture to say that those of us who have mastered the art of airbrushing would be loath to return to ordinary brushing for a number of reasons. However, before stating them, we might take a brief look at the equipment itself.

Airbrushes are miniature spray guns that first appeared on the scene in 1892 and were used mainly for photographic retouching. They are still used for this purpose but they are now also used for airbrush painting, custom car spraying, cake decoration, etc, etc. Those of you who can, like me, remember the 'Varga' girls of the war era have looked at airbrush work par excellence. (For those of you who are too young, Alberto Varga produced pin-ups of rather stylised, very pneumatic, semi-clad young ladies for the delectation of the armed forces and anybody else who was around.)

Whereas in scale model aircraft the artistic use of an airbrush may be required, eg mottled camouflage, in our field the emphasis is more likely to be on the plain, straightforward spraying aspect.

Going back to the advantages of the airbrush I would say that they are:

1. Speed — coverage is achieved quickly, given the right equipment, and the airbrush easily covers complicated shapes which are difficult to negotiate with an ordinary brush.
2. A 'clean cut' finish is more easily achieved. The great snags of brush painting — brushmarks and paint being pulled out by excrescences – are totally avoided and therefore 'detail clogging' does not occur.
3. Much less rubbing down is required, provided the paint is clean and/or well strained. Dust settling problems are also much reduced as diluted materials dry faster. They also give a reduced gloss even when high gloss materials are used, which I find an advantage (although wild horses will not induce me to enter into the argument as to whether models should be matt, semi-matt, semi-gloss or high gloss and that's the truth!)
4. Because of (3), less paint usually needs to be applied and this helps with the 'clean cut' appearance.

Airbrushes require a clean, dry air supply (or rather air or an *inert gas*) at about 30psi. Paasche recommend between 20 and 40psi according to the airbrush used. Various sources of compressed gas *can* be used; CO_2 cylinders, pumped up tyres, aerosol containers, full sized compressors, special airbrush compressors and a friend even used a tyre pump and air receiver. The fact is that serious airbrushing does require a compressor — any other source is likely to be too expensive or too inconvenient and both these considerations will prevent the full use of the instrument.

TYPES OF AIRBRUSHES

Airbrushes are basically of two types, single action and double action, the latter giving a more flexible control of application but being usually more expensive and requiring more skill to use properly.

Single action airbrushes. These have a valve controlling the air supply and hence the liquid being sprayed. Some have a needle valve that is separately (and manually) adjusted to control the spray pattern, but this is independent of the air valve. The Badger 200 is of this type and with this gun the spray size can also be reduced by only partially operating the air valve. This model is a good one for the average modeller.

Double action airbrushes. The valve on these types is pushed down for air control and pulled back for liquid control. This double action demands an acquired skill for proper and effective use and is the kind most favoured by airbrush experts.

There are a large number of airbrushes to select from, and really one's own requirements need to be defined accurately before purchase, not only as to whether a single action or double action brush is best, but also as to what liquids you expect to handle. Some airbrushes will only handle inks, water colour, etc, so it is essential to get one capable of spraying heavier materials if that is what you want. The cheapest airbrushes are usually of the external-mixing type, whereas the more expensive models mix the paint and air internally.

In brief — given that the handling capacity is great enough — the single action type is usually adequate for covering large areas, and it is cheaper. Use a double action brush for more fancy work as the amount sprayed (and the spray pattern) can be instantly and constantly altered. In addition, some airbrushes can be altered by changing the multi-head and needle, thus making the unit even more flexible.

USING THE AIRBRUSH

The successful use of an airbrush really requires a fastidious mentality. To say great care is needed is obvious when one looks at the price. The equipment is expensive because precision articles are involved, and they rely on that precision to work. Bent needles and bores needlessly reamed out with that handy piece of baling wire are not at all conducive to proper operation, and it is best not to keep an airbrush in the drawer with tools such as files. It must be kept clean and no paint should be left to harden off in the tip. Some workers even spray two-part epoxies and the like; the effect of these curing in the airbrush does not need to be spelt out.

Coarsely-ground paints may have pigment size approaching the sizes of the clearances in the airbrush and these must be avoided otherwise clogging will occur. This is particularly relevant if the paint passages are lined with hardened paint. *Any* dirt or skin in the paint supply will also inevitably block up the brush, so careful straining through a peice of gauze material is an absolute must, although paint from a newly-opened tin is usually satisfactory.

The degree of dilution for any material can only be gauged by experience and is dependent upon the viscosity of the material and what viscosity the airbrush can handle. I normally add about 50 per cent thinners to the paint as a starter — this is rarely too much. If the dilution is too great the airbrush will spray but no coverage will result; too low a dilution usually means, in extreme cases, no spray, or only a restricted amount. All that can be said is that the paint needs to be quite 'runny'.

Most airbrushes are sold with a booklet of lessons so that the beginner can teach himself the technique as well as instructions on cleaning and handling the instrument. The cleaning instructions should be followed closely since unnecessary dismantling of the gun should be avoided; however, inadequate cleaning will eventually require dismantling to remove hardened paint. Those using cellulose paints are better off as cellulose thinners are more 'self-cleaning' than the white spirit used with paints and enamels. You never see a skin over a cellulose paint for that reason.

My own arrangement for airbrushing is that I use both my Badger 200 (single action) and my Paasche VLS (double action) directly connected to my 2½ cu ft/min compressor, and allow the excess air to exhaust through the safety valve; although wasteful of air this system works very well and has the added advantage that the compressor is large enough to run a full-sized airgun as well. The air passes through a separator to remove any oil and water from the air before entering the airbrush airline. It is essential to remove these two substances from the air; they would otherwise contaminate the paint. You can buy an 'in-line' separator to fit directly in the airline and this is a sound investment.

I also keep a sealed tin of cellulose thinners for cleaning jars. This acts as a paint stripper for paints (dopes) and can be used over and over again.

Probably the last point to be borne in mind is the kind of paint container used. Some airbrushes use a gravity feed cup which will use up all the paint put in it. Suction-feed cups holding a restricted supply are also used, as are glass jars. These always have some paint left over below the suction pipe which is usually wasted.

SUMMARY

In conclusion, airbrushes are expensive and with a compressor even more so. However, as a finishing instrument they are second to none. I find that most expenditure on models is not on materials but on working equipment and this is always amortized over a number of models anyway. On that basis the cost of a superb finish is reasonable. As Ruskin said, 'All works of taste must bear a price in proportion to the skill, taste, time, expense and risk attending their manufacture. Those things called dear are, when justly estimated, the cheapest'. And that should be put up over every workbench.

No prices for airbrushing equipment have been given as these may well be out of date before publication and would only apply to the UK anyway.

Next issue I will write about the problems of masking, painting and masking being the 'Scylla and Charybdis' of finishing, as it were.

Above: the mediaeval harbour crane and the adjacent building now house the Polish Maritime Museum in Gdansk. *(All photographs by courtesy of the Polish Maritime Museum).*

THE POLISH MARITIME MUSEUM

by Ing Jerzy Litwin

This Maritime Museum in Gdansk is one of the youngest museums in Poland. It was established through the initiative of the Society of Friends of the Maritime Museum in Gdansk, which was formed in 1958 and had as its aim the calling into being of the Maritime Museum.

The exhibition 'From the Oar to Nuclear Propulsion', which was organised in 1959, became the nucleus of the Museum, and the Maritime Museum itself was founded on 1 October 1960 as a branch of the Gdansk Pomeranian Museum. Two years later the museum was given its independence, and at the same time moved into new premises — the historic building which used to house the mediaeval harbour crane and is now rebuilt after suffering war damage. In 1972 the museum was granted the name and status of Central Maritime Museum, thus becoming the leading establishment of its kind in Poland.

Doc dr hab Przemyslaw Smolarek, the founder of the Museum, was appointed manager, and he is still carrying out the duties of that office today. Right from the early preparatory days of the museum he advanced ideas and general guidelines for the collecting of exhibits. These principles, as it later turned out, were far ahead of those prevailing in the majority of European maritime museums.

The realization of the programme for putting together the collections has not been an easy task, handicapped as it was by two world

wars and the earlier 123-year period of the partition of Poland among three bordering countries. This caused a considerable dispersal of the works of art, and created a gap in Polish culture.

The earliest attempt to establish a maritime museum in Poland came after World War I, when one was opened in Warsaw in 1924 by its founder and proprietor Count Stanislaw Ledochowski. World War II caused further destruction to and dispersal of nautical monuments, among these being the above-mentioned pioneer establishment in Warsaw. In 1945 when the old Slavonic territories, reaching as far as the River Oder, were restored to Poland, new prospects opened up for the development of maritime museums on the long wide zone bordering the Polish sea coast. The first such museum was organised at Szczecinie, and it is still in existence there today, though in a somewhat reorganised form as the Maritime Department of the multi-directional National Museum. In 1953 a Naval Museum was established in Gdynia. At that time these two museums provided safe keeping for all the nautical material available in Poland.

The much later Maritime Museum in Gdansk has had to direct its activities to searching for exhibits in the antique markets, as well as to the underwater exploration of wrecks of old ships — a never-failing source for worthwhile material. Ship models for the most part until now have been obtained either by purchase or as gifts from private individuals or from firms in the

Top: model of a mediaeval boat discovered at Mechlinki near Gdynia.
Centre: model of a *berlinka* — a ship used to carry goods on the river Vistula and the river Oder in the 18th century.
Bottom: one of the Museum's most recent purchases, a model of the Polish built cargo training ship *Antoni Garnuszewski*.

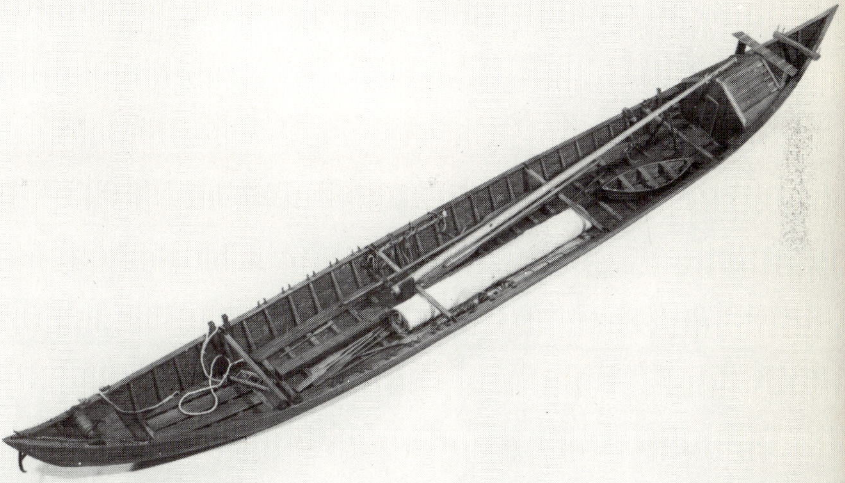

maritime industry.

Today, after 18 years, the number of ship models in the collection exceeds 300, covering a wide range of categories. The most valuable among them is a collection of 15 old models which includes a Mediterranean felucca from about 1576, the oldest model in the collection. That model, together with the two-decker *St Jacob* from the seventeenth century and the eighteenth century vessel *Den Heldenmodige,* belonged to the collection which, up to 1945, had been kept in the Artus' Court in Gdansk.

Other collections consist of models produced more recently, among which is a group of specially built models of early/mediaeval Slavonic boats at 1/10 scale and — a rarity in European museums — a series of mediaeval ships such as the cog and the holk, all to 1/50 scale.

Another class of vessel which played an important part in the history of Polish shipping were the inland waterway ships used to carry goods up to Gdansk on the river Vistula. The following types were used for this traffic during the sixteenth to nineteenth centuries: szkuta, dubas, galar, komiega, and berinka. Models of these boats have been built to a scale of 1/25, their construction being based among other things on plans dating from 1792. The collections of ship models are supplemented by reconstructions of vessels from the seventeenth and eighteenth centuries (such as the first galleon, the *Smok/Dragon,* launched in 1571 by two Venetian masters

23

Top: model of a fishing vessel, the *taglerpolte,* used on the Szczecin Lagoon up to the 20th century.
Bottom: model of a Mediterranean felucca the second half of the 16th century.
(Photo courtesy of P Simson).

invited to Poland and later used in the regular Polish Navy created by King Zygmunt August) and by models of galleons and fluits from the time of the victorious Battle of Oliva in 1627. A systematic exploration of the Swedish warship *Solen*, which blew up during this battle, is now being carried out by members of the Polish Maritime Museum. Another project is the construction of a group of models of the ships on which Joseph Conrad sailed; three of them, the *Torrens, Roi des Belges* and *Vidar,* have been completed.

Ships of modern times are represented by two collections. The first consists of models of vessels from the period 1920-1945, while the other comprises models of vessels launched after 1945. The many models in these two groups, completed or yet to be finished, are to a scale of 1/100.

Although I have dealt with the models of warships and merchant ships in the Polish Maritime Museum, I must also mention the collection of models of local ship types and of fishing boats in the Fishery Branch at Hel. The Gdansk museum also contains a series of models of vessels found outside Europe, for example local types from Indonesia and Bangladesh.

For the past two years the museum has had a model workship, the main task of which is model building and preservation work, and in due course it will be supplying the museum with new exhibits.

Above: *Pintail* in drydock at Falmouth early in 1979. This photograph was taken on the day she docked, and the weed and other fouling on the shell has not been cleared. Nevertheless the general lines of the hull can be seen. This is rather an historic photograph as *Pintail* was one of the last vessels to dock in Falmouth drydock, as British Shipbuilders (at the time of writing – May 1979) had decided to close the docks the following month. *(Photograph reproduced by courtesy of Packet Newspapers, proprietors of the* **Falmouth Packet**).

BACK TO THE DRAWING BOARD
by Brian Stevens

My interest was caught by the photograph of *Mandarin* in the article on Boom Defence Vessels by Mr P N Thomas in the June 1977 issue of *Model Shipwright*, one of the articles he has written under the title of 'Ships That Served'.

Mandarin, with her sister ship *Pintail*, was completed by Cammell Laird on Merseyside in 1964. More rightly they are described nowadays as Mooring, Salvage and Boom Defence Vessels (MSBDV). At that time I was working in the Design Office at Laird's and along with a senior designer, Bill Mellor, was given the job of designing these two ships to a specification drawn up by MOD(N). This was done for almost all ships in the 'enquiry' stage, and in this case Laird's was one of a number of yards tendering for the work. Detailed initial design was necessary to allow the Estimating Office to cost the work from the quantities of materials which we would lift from our completed design. These included steel, deck coverings, castings, tiling, piping, paint, timber, insulation and bulkhead cladding.

TENDERING

In this early stage only a preliminary general arrangement plan was circulated by the Owners, MOD(N) in this case, to all shipyards tendering. One had to modify this, trying for the optimum solution and keeping the final cost down, to allow one's own shipyard a chance of winning the contract. The original internal layout of the accommodation on the preliminary general arrangement plan seemed very haphazard to us, trained as we were to make the most of space in everyday merchant ship contracts. Setting out to right this, we came up with a plan which cut passageways and the doglegs in them to a minimum, so increasing crew cabin sizes and giving good shapes to each cabin. In the event the original design was reinstituted when the ships were built. I never did find out why — could it have been that crews preferred a more homely clutter? Anyway, I will not admit to having much to do with structure above the upper deck!

Among the more unusual tasks to be carried out for this particular design was a three-dimensional drawing of the horns and bow apron. This was to enable the necessary internal stiffening to be worked out. The drawing proved of further use when the ship Drawing Office was making the working drawings for the shipyard.

Cammell Laird did win the contract for the two vessels (yard nos 1310 and 1311). Needless to say we were very pleased. At that time the company was averaging a success rate of about one contract in every five enquiries.

PRODUCTION DESIGN

In 1963 the use of the computer in ship hull design was in its infancy and so hull lines and all the associated calculations were worked out manually. Actually, our ship Design Office had already started to use the DANSK computer in Denmark under the guidance of our Naval Architect, Ralph Downham. This was used only to check basic calculations. One still had the satisfaction of drawing the lines and shaping the hull to get displacement, centre of buoyancy and powering right, yet at the same time feeling that the art of producing a fair hull was still something that came from within one's self, rather than from the dead figures of the present day perfecting computer. Of course it used to take days using manual methods and I am speaking of only sixteen years ago.

With these ships there was a considerable penalty if we failed to achieve the required stability when completed. This penalty could have gone as far as full rejection, had too much discrepancy resulted. Whilst our initial calculations showed that with their specified beam dimension each ship would just achieve this requirement, such ships do have a habit of collecting extra top hamper during construction. It was decided that the beam should be increased slightly from the start. The extra cost of the hull steel would not be significant and certainly less than any penalty we should have to pay for not achieving the minimum acceptable measure of stability. With the design parameters laid down, everything was ready to start drawing.

Although I had worked previously, in conjunction with others, on car ferry and tanker lines plans, the lines plan for the future *Mandarin* and *Pintail* was only large enough for one designer to work on, drawn as it was to a scale of ¼in = 1ft. The first process was to cut linen-backed cartridge paper from the roll and lay it out on the long flat drawing board to stretch and stabilise at room temperature overnight.

Trying to draw the basic framework of baseline and station positions too quickly would have caused inaccuracies following the usual shrinkage as the paper subsequently dried out in a warm office. When one is working to a scale of ¼in = 1ft, it is so easy to lose inches in full size when lifting station offsets later, from a plan which has shrunk almost unnoticeably in the first day or so of drawing.

Every Naval Architect will have experienced the pleasure of anticipation when faced with a clean sheet of paper from which a ship's hull shape would grow. It may seem rather nonsensical to admit to this feeling when writing about the hull lines of a heavy workship, rather than those of, say, a fast car ferry, but that was just the feeling at the time. There has always seemed to be enough ugliness designed into our everyday lives, and here was a chance to make a more positive contribution. It was with this thought in mind that I set out to give the vessels the best lines possible within the scope allowed.

DRAWING THE LINES PLAN

After pinning the stretched paper, the next operation was to lay down the baseline of the profile and body plan, with the middle line for the waterlines below. We had a standard method of laying out a lines plan of profile set above the plan view of waterlines, with the body plan at the left hand end of the profile's extended baseline. The profile was drawn with the bow to the right hand (figure 1).

As this is probably the only plan drawn in shipbuilding from which working dimensions are measured directly, set-squares and tee-squares do not produce sufficient accuracy when drawing right-angles and parallel lines. Therefore all of the basic framework of the lines plan was constructed using simple geometry. For accuracy the base line was set up by stretching cotton between two pins. Using a very sharp 2H pencil, fine marks were made just under the cotton, at about 6in intervals. The base and waterline centrelines were then inked in using a machined steel straightedge.

The straightedge was not used without the initial pencilled check marks as it was difficult to hold the drawing pen at the same angle throughout the long stroke. Change of pen angle would have produced a gently waving and therefore inaccurate baseline. The forward and aft perpendiculars were constructed in the usual geometrical way, using drawing bows (compasses) set at their greatest open angle and with the pencil lead sharpened to a chisel point. Incidentally the best way to sharpen a pencil is to cut away the wood, leaving about 12mm (½in) of lead exposed, and then rub the lead against a very fine file (rather than sandpaper). With this method any shape of point can be quickly made or resharpened. Keep the file in some handy open container as a lot of graphite dust collects very quickly and can soon spread over fingers and plan. Striking arcs which crossed each other, above and below the baseline, produced crossing points which, when joined together, themselves produced accurate perpendiculars. In fact in this case trammels were used rather than bows, as one could then make full use of their long reach to improve accuracy.

You will have noticed that whilst the baseline has been mentioned the keel line has not. On most large ships

they coincide, but on many smaller craft the keel is raked down from bow to stern, so helping to keep the propeller as deep as possible under all conditions. Such was the case with this craft. The moulded keel line was drawn in, passing through the midship station and giving a reduction in draught at the forward perpendicular and a corresponding increase aft.

Using the aft perpendiculars as Station 0 and the forward perpendicular as Station 10 the other Stations 1 to 9 were spaced at 1/10 of the ship length apart. Half-stations were added at 1½ and 8½. Between Station 0 and 1, and between 9 and 10, quarter-stations were also constructed.

Stations and frame positions do not necessarily coincide and as the actual frame spacing and frame positions are not required at such an early stage of hull shaping they are not normally drawn on the lines plan. The station lines were all extended to cover the plan view of the lines below (figure 1).

The verticals giving the moulded breadth of the ship were drawn on the body plan. The left hand side of the middle line would show the after body stations, ie Station 5 (midships) to Station 0; the right hand side of the plan would show the fore body

stations, ie Station 5 (midships) to station 10. It will be noted that Station 5 (midships) always appears on both sides and acts as a good transition reference for both half-bodies.

The bilge radius was then chosen and together with the rise of floor line was drawn on both sides of the body plan. The rise of floor is the upward rake of the bottom plating from the edges of the keelplate — usually totally flat for the majority of its length and breadth — and the turn of bilge. In ships, this rake serves two main puposes. First, it allows liquids to drain to the centreline for pumping purposes. Second, during the drydocking operation it ensures that the stiffened keel area touches the blocks first and there is then less chance of the blocks placed outboard damaging the relatively unstiffened outboard areas of hull bottom plating. The outboard or bilge blocks are hardened up with wooden wedges when the dock is dry.

Attention then moved back to the profile drawing and the stem and stern frames were drawn relative to the forward and aft perpendiculars. The size of the propeller aperture in the stern frame was quite a critical factor. In the early 1960s a lot of

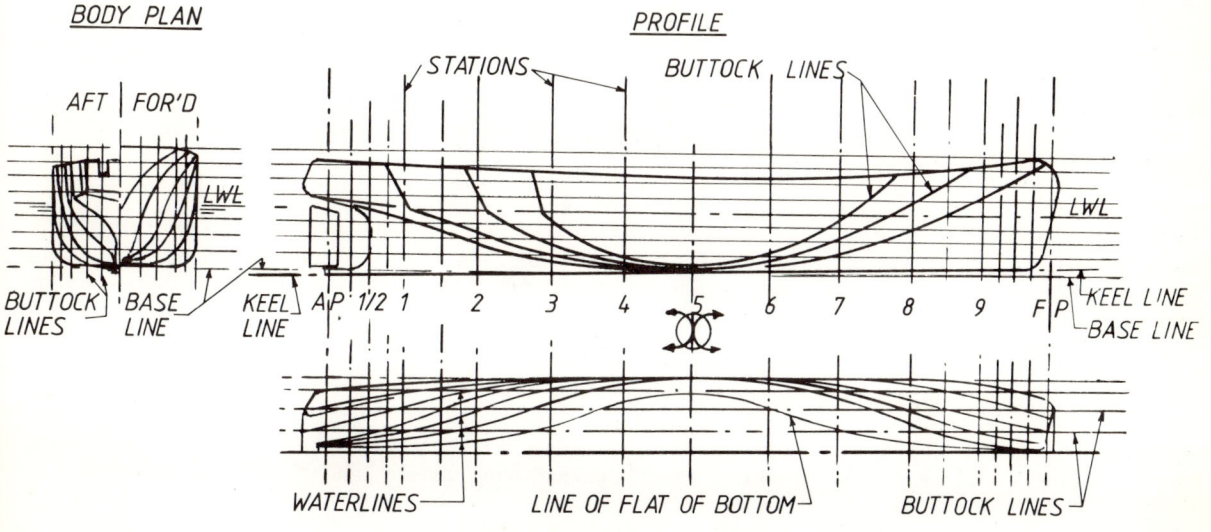

BODY PLAN   PROFILE

FIG 1   TYPICAL LAYOUT OF LINES AND BODY PLAN
                              (NOT TO SCALE)

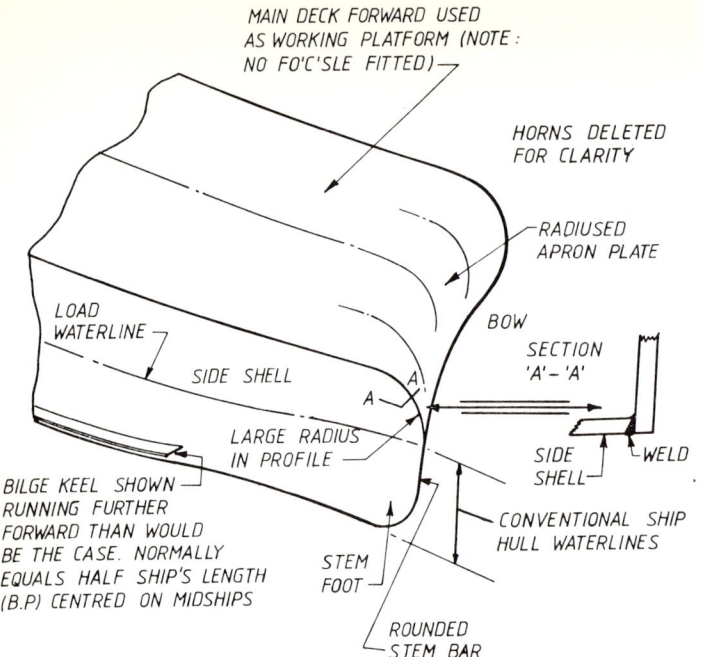

MAIN DECK FORWARD USED AS WORKING PLATFORM (NOTE: NO FO'C'SLE FITTED)

HORNS DELETED FOR CLARITY

RADIUSED APRON PLATE

LOAD WATERLINE

SIDE SHELL

BOW

SECTION 'A'-'A'

A'

A

LARGE RADIUS IN PROFILE

SIDE SHELL

WELD

BILGE KEEL SHOWN RUNNING FURTHER FORWARD THAN WOULD BE THE CASE. NORMALLY EQUALS HALF SHIP'S LENGTH (B.P) CENTRED ON MIDSHIPS

CONVENTIONAL SHIP HULL WATERLINES

STEM FOOT

ROUNDED STEM BAR

FIG 2

research had been carried out to achieve the best clearances between propeller and stern frame and the results were used when deciding the shape of the *Mandarin/Pintail* stern aperture.

Stern overhang and the transom shape were dictated by the operational aspects of workboat duties, which would involve two relatively heavy anchors worked over the stern. In effect, the result in both profile and transom views improved the stern looks of these ships when compared with the *Bar* class vessels. More about the stern later.

The bow and stem, too, had particular shape, to suit working rather than sea conditions. As the forward part of the main deck was also a broad working platform there was a conflict in having a broad deckline tapering quickly in plan view to a conventional ship shape at the waterline (figure 2). One can often achieve this in some craft by introducing a knuckle above the waterline, which allows a sharp change of contour. This was not a satisfactory solution for four reasons. First, a lot of work with wires and cables would be done over the side and such a sharp contour would cause unnecessary wear. It could also have fouled items during an

overside lift. (I note with interest that part of the sheerstrake of the latest class represented by *Pochard* is radiused into the deck, making overside working even easier. This was not a requirement of the original *Wild Duck* class). The second reason was a combination of the achievement of more comfortable working and sailing conditions. These ships would often work in areas where conditions give short but steep seas. Because of their relatively short length and broad beam they could, under some conditions, pitch appreciably. Given a smooth nodding motion, the crew could more easily work on the fore deck. A knuckle would have produced a jerking pitch when the ship's head went into the water, the extra flare giving the effect of sudden increase in buoyancy during the forward pitching movement. Thirdly, pronounced flare would also have increased the panting effect on the forward hull when underway, making her an uncomfortable ship in which to sail — or rest when off watch! Finally, a knuckle, directly under the anchor pocket, could give rise to the flukes jamming under the knuckle when weighing anchor.

So *Mandarin/Pintail* were given a soft radius to the stem foot and conventional waterlines up to the

point at which the stem met the bottom point of the flat apron plate. The latter swept round from the deck over the entire bow width in a large radius forming a right-angle, port and starboard, at the meeting between apron edge and side shell plating (figure 2). This one hard-spot on the bow was almost unavoidable but in practice should have had little effect on working performance as the heavy lifts over the bow usually take place with the lifting wires running between the horns. The apron radius over the bow was made large to allow the wires a gentle run when supporting an overbow load. As with most salvage vessels, the ship herself can be used as a lifting tool. Filling ballast tanks forward puts her head deep and after securing the heavy lift on the sea bed over the bow, the tanks are pumped out. This lifts the ship, which then moves to shallower water, carrying its load until the latter grounds again on the sea bed. Used in unison with the extra tidal lift available up to high tide, appreciable progress in the recovery of heavy items can be made. I would not pretend to be any kind of expert in the use of salvage ships, but I am sure that there are a legion of tunes one can play with such instruments.

At the point at which the conventional stem meets the waterline there is a reverse knuckle which is hardly noticeable. In effect the idea was to try and keep the apron just clear of the water under normal sailing conditions in moderate seas, but there is no compromise possible when the ship is taking it green over the bows. That the initial object was achieved can be seen from the photograph on page 324 of *Model Shipwright* No 20 showing almost no bow wave. The apron is obviously taking a skim of water, which is blown aft as it runs off the sideshell knuckle, but is not of consequence in making resistance. Of more concern in this context would be the second plume of water which can be seen about 20ft aft of the bow. This is caused by the heavy timber side sheathing similar to that shown on the *Bar* class plans. However, these vessels are primarily workboats, spending much of their time almost stationary, and one accepts that speed and resistance are not prime factors.

The line of sheer at the deck edge is a product of the line of sheer at the middle line of the main deck, associated with the thwartships deck camber (figure 3). The sheerline stands out well in the photograph and still pleases the eye.

PRELIMINARY BODY PLAN

With the main profile fixed, a start was made on a preliminary body plan using tracing paper covering the original. This was sketched in freehand, only the bilge radius on Station 5 having been fixed, as mentioned earlier. Each of the ten stations was sketched in, five on the left hand side giving the forebody and five on the right giving the afterbody, with additional half-stations at bow and stern. My personal preference for modifying the fullness of a hull has always been to use the bilge diagonal in the early stages. It is easy to lift off half-breadths down a diagonal and draw a curve of these lengths on a foreshortened base line (figure 4). Any basic fairing required immediately shows up.

Using an instrument called a planimeter it was simple to roughly check the areas produced on the sketch body plan and, putting them through Simpson's Rule, work out a volume of underwater hull and hence convert to displacement in tons. The first result gave 1045 tons if my memory serves me correctly. It was necessary to pare another 95 tons from this to get to the desired 950 tons. Having the area at each station and its distance relative to midships it was possible also to check the longitudinal centre of buoyancy. This proved to be almost where required and so all that was left to do was to slim down the hull by an equal amount in both fore and aft bodies. This would leave the centre of buoyancy in the correct position. I seem to remember that we aimed to get this point about 1-1½ per cent of length forward of midships. This would ensure a slight fullness of body forward, compared with aft, which helped the hull to lift a little in forward motion at sea. Of course the estimated longitudinal centre of gravity of the completed ship had to be balanced also, to give only designed trim in the operating

condition, and this too had a bearing on the position of the centre of buoyancy.

A new bilge diagonal curve (B in figure 4) was run inside the original on the foreshortened base line and the lengths transferred back to the body plan. Each station was then fined down to pass through its revised point and the process of checking done again. This immediately showed how much had been shaved from the excess 95 tons. It also gave a very good indication of how far the next bilge diagonal curve would need to be run inside the first diagonal, by looking at the proportion of areas already removed, against the lost tonnage. In fact the third bilge diagonal checks (C) gave almost exactly the volume of displacement required, including a small margin.

The rough body plan was then hardened up using ship body curves. I have a favourite curve which even today still seems to fit all the situations I ask of it. Moulded Volume of Displacement and the position of the centre of buoyancy were then checked again. The half-breadths lifted from the body were

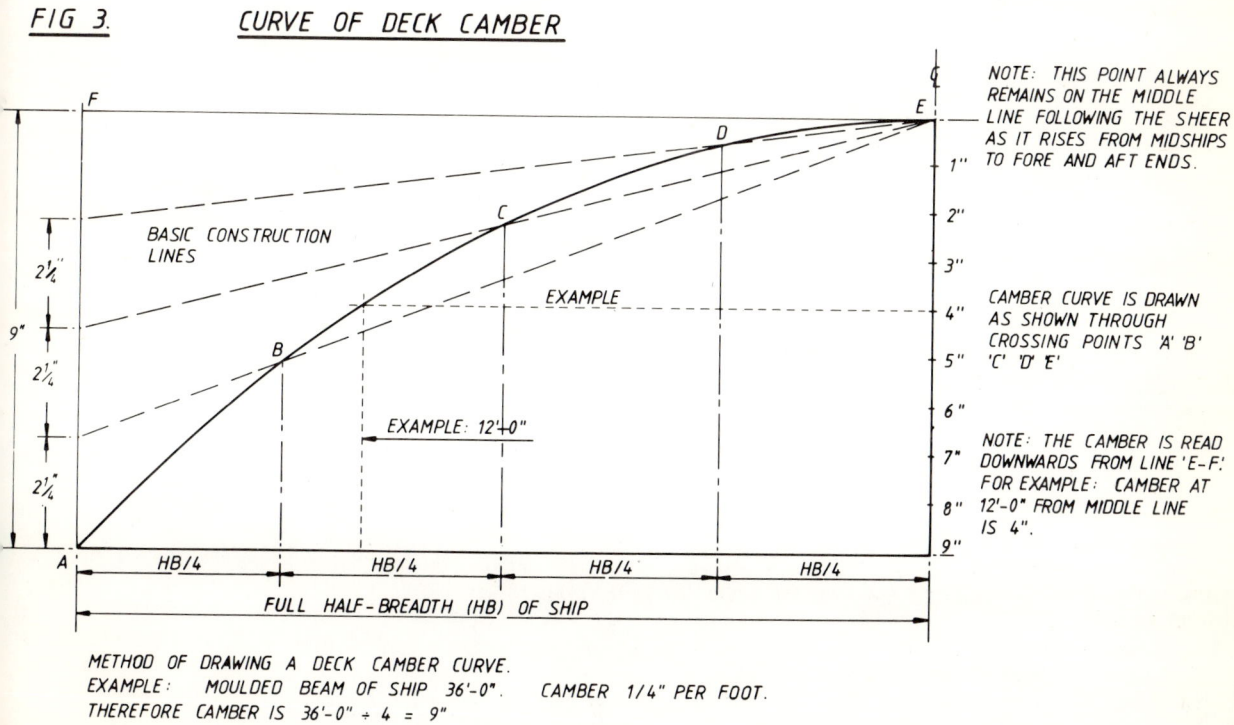

FIG 3.   CURVE OF DECK CAMBER

NOTE: THIS POINT ALWAYS REMAINS ON THE MIDDLE LINE FOLLOWING THE SHEER AS IT RISES FROM MIDSHIPS TO FORE AND AFT ENDS.

CAMBER CURVE IS DRAWN AS SHOWN THROUGH CROSSING POINTS 'A' 'B' 'C' 'D' 'E'

NOTE: THE CAMBER IS READ DOWNWARDS FROM LINE 'E-F'. FOR EXAMPLE: CAMBER AT 12'-0" FROM MIDDLE LINE IS 4".

BASIC CONSTRUCTION LINES

EXAMPLE

EXAMPLE: 12'-0"

FULL HALF-BREADTH (HB) OF SHIP

METHOD OF DRAWING A DECK CAMBER CURVE.
EXAMPLE: MOULDED BEAM OF SHIP 36'-0".   CAMBER 1/4" PER FOOT.
THEREFORE CAMBER IS 36'-0" ÷ 4 = 9"

then transferred to the working lines plan and lines pencilled in to check their run. Slight variations were smoothed out using a long pear-wood batten, bending it to the stations through which it would comfortably run.

It is good practice when doing this to use never less than four stations (figure 5). After placing the batten and holding it in position at each station using weights, lift each weight in turn, starting from the next-but-one nearest midships. This allows any inbuilt error to be taken out, as the batten will spring slightly into a fair curve once the weight is lifted. The new half-breadth at any station where this correction has occurred should then be transferred to the body plan. Beware of excessive differences or considerable movement of the batten when released, as you could be building errors into the body plan. Good battens should be made of straight-grained wood or plastic strip in lengths suitable for comfortable handling and roughly

$\frac{1}{8}$in thick throughout, having one end about $\frac{1}{4}$in wide tapering to $\frac{1}{8}$in at the other. When putting the batten on the lines plan, the thick end should be at or towards midships. If the hull form being drawn has very little flat of side, the lines should be run with batten covering the station beyond midships (figure 5), so that one does not finish up with a peak at this point, which will occur if lines of both fore and aft bodies are started right on the midship station. When a batten has been sprung and appears to have taken a fair line, go to one end of the plan and sight along the batten. If this view is foreshortened by keeping the eye near to the plan surface, any discrepancies are more easily seen. Adjust the batten accordingly.

If possible the weights used should each be attached to a firm hardwood base which has a working end coming almost to a point (figure 6) — this will allow the greatest pressure possible to be put on the batten at a station. Hence

the need for the lifting of weights in sequence to produce a fair line. Particular care should be taken when a batten is curved, perhaps in three directions. This will occur on the full hulls of smaller ships (figure 5), with the batten sweeping out, say, to cross from Station 6 to Station 5 (amidships) and then back in at Stations 4 and 3 and cut again through 2, 1 and 0 (the aft perpendicular). Where the lines run close together and almost parallel, it is easy to accept what appear to be small errors but these have a significant effect when the buttock lines are drawn. Particular care is also required on modern hulls where the run under the counter is very flat. It is even possible for many lines to be run in plan view — each apparently fair — through the after stations. It is in circumstances like these that buttock lines come into their own.

Buttock lines are most important, although many amateur designers find them a nuisance when, to all intents and purposes, the body plan,

Barlow, built in 1938 by Wm Simons Ltd, Renfrew.

FIG 4

INITIAL FAIRING AND DISPLACEMENT CHECKS USING THE BILGE DIAGONALS

PRELIMINARY BODY PLAN
(NOT TO SCALE)
CURVE OF BILGE DIAGONALS
A
B
C
1ST CHECK
2ND CHECK
0 1 2 3 4 5 6 7 8 9 10
ROF
BILGE DIAGONAL
EXAMPLE SHOWN AT STATION 6 ONLY

FIG 5

METHOD OF HOLDING & DRAWING AROUND THE BATTEN.

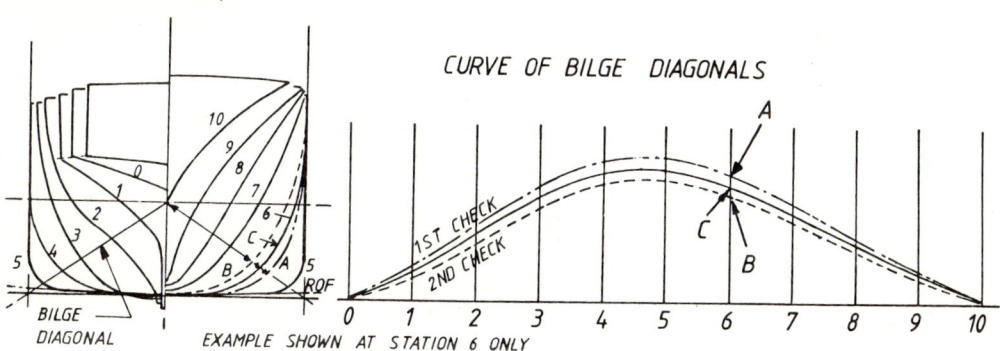

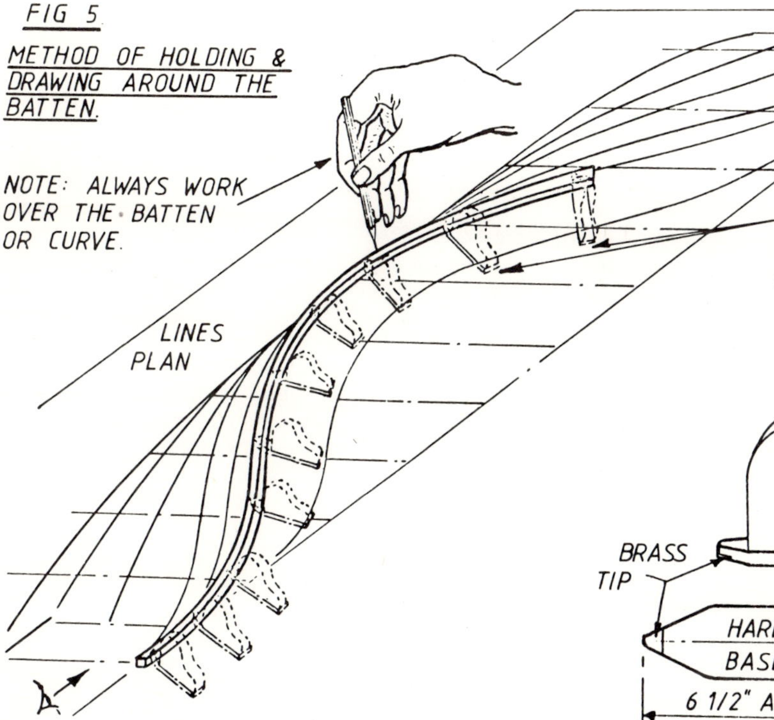

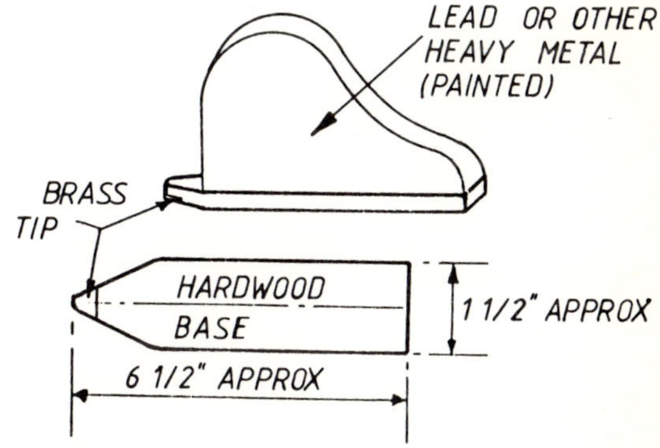

NOTE: ALWAYS WORK OVER THE BATTEN OR CURVE.
APPROXIMATE POSITIONS OF WEIGHTS HOLDING BATTEN.
LINES PLAN

LEAD OR OTHER HEAVY METAL (PAINTED)
BRASS TIP
HARDWOOD BASE
1 1/2" APPROX
6 1/2" APPROX

FIG 6 TYPICAL BATTEN WEIGHT

FIG 7

METHOD OF DETERMINING RUDDER AREA

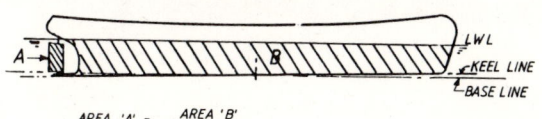

A
B
LWL
KEEL LINE
BASE LINE

$$AREA\ 'A' = \frac{AREA\ 'B'}{45}$$

lines and profile have the appearance of being fair. On box-like hulls with a great deal of flat of side and bottom, such as tankers, buttocks are often drawn only for the ends. Indeed in some cases whole segments of the hull amidships may not appear on the lines plan at all.

The buttock lines appear on the profile drawing itself (figure 1) and use heights above the base, lifted at such station at stipulated distances from the middle line of the ship. When these points are joined on the profile, the fairness or otherwise of the hull becomes apparent immediately. With buttocks particularly, it will be found that the quite large vertical variations of the line needed to produce a fair line will result in only small adjustments on the body or lines plan. Nevertheless, it gives one real satisfaction in completing a plan which has all these views in agreement.

RUDDER DESIGN
No hull design would be complete without the inclusion of a means of steering, and some notes on rudder design would be appropriate at this point. In general the area of the rudder is recognised as a function of the area of the underwater profile of the hull itself.

This varies according to the type

Below: *Barlane*, built in 1937 by Lobnitz & Co Ltd, Renfrew.
(Photos by courtesy of P N Thomas).

of ship and size involved, but usually falls between 1/40 and 1/50 of this profile area. In certain cases, as with fast liners, the area can be reduced to about 1/85. Our target was about 1/45 (figure 7). To be effective a rudder should be as deep as possible without excessive length. Fortunately there was space to get a good depth of rudder between the underside of the counter and the keel line. Dividing the ideal area required by this depth produced a fore and aft dimension which gave the rudder a rectangular shape, auguring well for the ships' handling qualities when built. The rudder was balanced with about 1/3 of the area ahead of the rudder stock, which would result in quick response to helm orders and an easily operated steering gear. The result was a simple rudder with a good area, yet still easy to service and remove for repair.

As with most vessels specifically designed for salvage operations and where rope will often be handled in the stem area, the propeller was protected with an open cage similar to that shown on the *Bar* class plan. What may be of interest is that this causes significant drag, interrupts streamline flow and can require an increase of up to 20 per cent in engine power to overcome their combined effects. Quite the reverse occurs when, as seen nowadays on many tugs and offshore craft, a fully shrouded propeller (such as the Kort Nozzle) is used.

TANK TESTING
In those days, offset information — in the form of a tracing of the body plan and profile — of each new hull design was sent from the yard to the National Physical Laboratory. This enabled them to prepare a model hull in wax and check resistance and powering by running the model, in various wave configurations, down their long test tank. They could then make suggestions, where necessary, for improving hull shape In this instance the hull shape was tested and apparently proved entirely satisfactory. This was very pleasing indeed as I had been particularly careful in trying to achieve a good run of lines in the afterbody, fining them off to the maximum to achieve the best waterflow possible to the propeller and help nullify the effect of the propeller cage.

Similarly lines forward, below the load waterline, were given a fine entrance and run, from the stem. All the effort had proved worthwhile and the lines as drawn would grow on the slipway into pleasing hulls, despite being only workboats. Hopefully their hulls at least would please the eye when underway and prove stable and comfortable for the men who would spend a considerable proportion of their lives working aboard in all weather conditions, often hove-to, but still rolling and pitching in offshore waters.

THE CARGO LINER
MATHURA

by James Pottinger

Above: *Mathura* under way. *(Photo courtesy of the Cunard Steamship Co Ltd.)*
Below: note the top of the heavy lift derrick at the forward bipod mast swathed in protective canvas. *Winneba* ex *Umgeni* lying astern.

The subject of these drawings was one of a fleet of general cargo vessels, with accommodation for a few passengers, owned by T & J Brocklebank Ltd of Liverpool, and which were the last of their later steam driven vessels.

This company was probably unique, outside America, in that they remained faithful to steam propulsion until 1963, when they took delivery of two Sulzer diesel-engined vessels built by Alexander Stephen & Sons Ltd, of Linthouse, Glasgow. Their only other incursion into the internal combustion field

was a lone vessel propelled by a Cammell-Fullagar engine, a slightly odd configuration whereby each crank was driven by two pistons, the upper piston in one cylinder driving one crank, the lower piston in the other cylinder being coupled to the same crank pin, and the upper piston driving through diagonal rods to the crossheads of the other adjacent connecting rod at the crosshead — in fact a forerunner to the well known opposed piston design. The normal arrangement now is for the upper pistons to be connected to the crank by means of side rods and eccentric journals on crank webs. This ship, the *Malia*, ran trials on the Clyde in September 1921, but did not remain long in service with Brocklebanks.

While conservative in many ways the company was in the forefront in certain developments being, among other things, the first British shipowners to employ AC current throughout. Valuable experience was gained on the *Maskeliya* of 1954 when two electric winches were

other companies.

The origins of the company go back to 1770, making them the oldest private shipowners in the world. However some years ago they became part of the Cunard group, along with the Port Line, and now are part of the Trafalgar House group of companies. With totally different trading operations the familiar blue and white funnel and house flag is noticeably absent from the maritime trade routes in comparison with previous years.

The *Mathura* was one of the many ships built for Brocklebanks by William Hamilton & Co Ltd at Port Glasgow (now part of the Scott-Lithgow Group) and was completed in 1960. She sailed on the Company's regular India, Ceylon and Red Sea ports routes, with occasional calls at Northern and Gulf ports in the USA, normally carrying general cargo outwards, often including steel and capital goods, and returning with jute, gunny, tea and sometimes ore from India, and with grain from the USA.

My early service with Brocklebanks as an engineer officer was on one of their oldest reciprocating-engined ships, and I can remember clambering through her engine room whilst she was fitting out as Greenock during one of my leaves, being in startling contrast to my previous ship, and although I did not serve on the *Mathura* I did coastwise voyages on the later sister *Mangla* and the older *Masirah*, the latter differing in that she was fitted with Scotch boilers instead of watertube boilers. The deck views which accompany this article were taken on the *Masirah* whilst in Tilbury Docks, and although this ship was not an exact sister the deck arrangements and fittings were basically similar, the main difference being that *Masirah's* funnel was mounted directly on the boat deck and appeared taller and more imposing than that on *Mathura* which was set on top of a deck-high casing. Incidentally the ship lying astern of the *Masirah* is the *Winneba* in Elder Dempster colours; she was formerly the *Umgeni* of the Bullard King Line, and was my first ship as an engineer prior to joining the Brocklebank Line.

operated on AC current to investigate methods of speed and hoisting control, the remainder of the winches being of steam type. The AC machinery in the engine room was backed up by steam standby units. The *Mangla* of 1959 was the first ship to go AC completely and was something of a novelty for the engineering staff initially until they became familiar with the plant. The company notched up another first when they became the first British owners to install bridge control of the engines; this was on the motor ships *Markhor* and *Mahout* built by Alexander Stephen & Sons Ltd in 1963. They were also among the earliest owners to fit bipod masts and GRP lifeboats.

There is a legend that Brocklebanks, alarmed by the number of ships being lost by surface gunfire in World War I , purchased a number of obsolete and surplus guns on their own account to arm their ships. Unverified too is the tale that some special dispensation was received to allow them to fly the blue and white house flag at the foremast instead of on the mizzenmast as is normal with all

Opposite top: close up of the stem, showing the curved shape of the stem plate, the circular port for the Suez Canal searchlight behind the house flag, and the square recess for the anchor. Note the fairleads in the bulwark.

Opposite bottom: looking aft from the bridge, showing details of the tops of the samson posts, the awning spars and stanchions of tubular steel, and the head of the sliding part of the boat davits.

Below left: looking forward from the monkey island. Note the construction of the top of the bipod masts, the bulwark stays, and shape of the masthouse curtain plates.

Below right: looking aft from the forecastle to show details of the front of the superstructure. Note that the guard rail stanchions are of heavy rectangular section flat bar, and not the more usual round forgings.

APPEARANCE DETAILS

The actual model should be sufficiently challenging for the more experienced modeller without presenting any undue difficulties. I will give a run down on some of the salient points about the ship. Starting forward we have a slightly curved and raked stem, with the radius being carried well down to the waterline. The Suez Canal searchlight was mounted on rails under the forecastle deck and on opening the circular port in the stem plate it could be run out into position ready for use; note the house flag painted on this port. The forecastle deck carries the usual anchor windlass and chain stoppers, and a bracket is fitted at the after end of the deck to house the derricks when these are in the lowered position.

The mast houses on the foredeck carry the electric cargo winches on top, with the bipod masts passing down through. Ladders are fitted to the outboard side of the masts, with an opening in the top plate of the mast crosstrees to provide access aloft; note the cross-section of the bipod masts — flat fore and aft but with convex curved sides.

The midship superstructure is carried on the raised centre castle and is quite lofty. It is surmounted by a well-proportioned funnel having a curved domed top, a forerunner of similar units fitted to the former Cunarders *Saxonia, Carinthia, Ivernia,* etc built by John Brown & Co at Clydebank. The top half of the funnel was removable to provide clearance when passing up the Manchester Ship Canal, and the

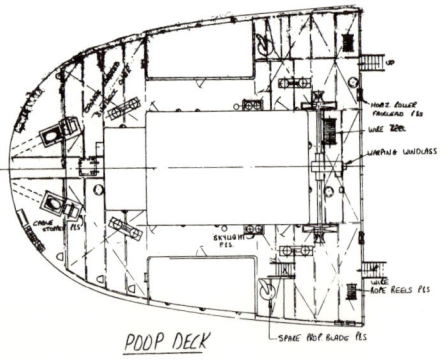

foremast top dropped down through the mast top. The radar mast was also portable, and could be temporarily transferred to a special mounting plate lower down on the bridge. At one time a number of the later Brocklebank ships adopted naval practice and carried whip aerials mounted at each side of the funnel, but these were prone to breakages due to rolling.

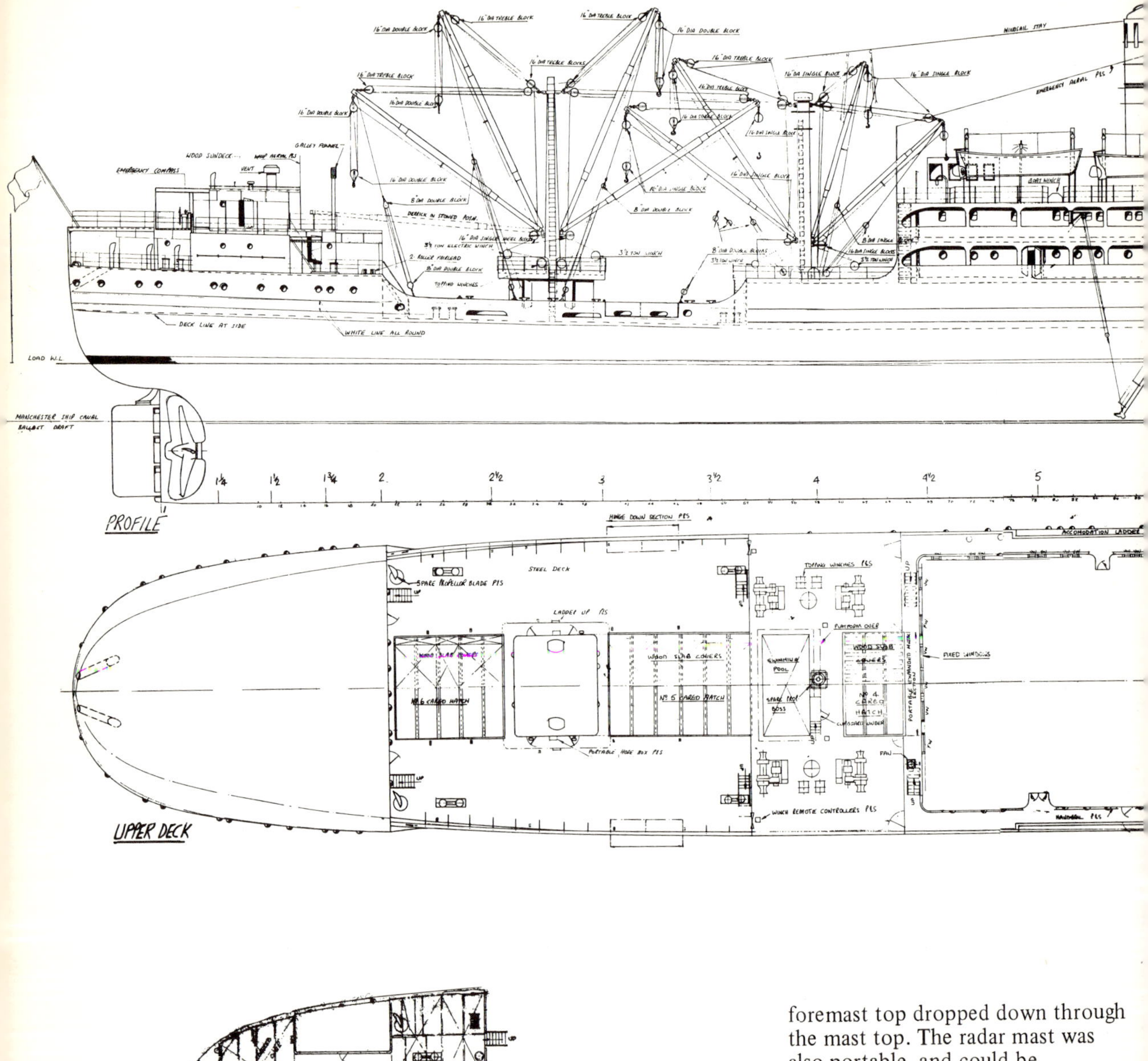

The lifeboats are carried high up, on gravity davits, with the fall winches underneath. No engine room skylight was fitted, a portable section

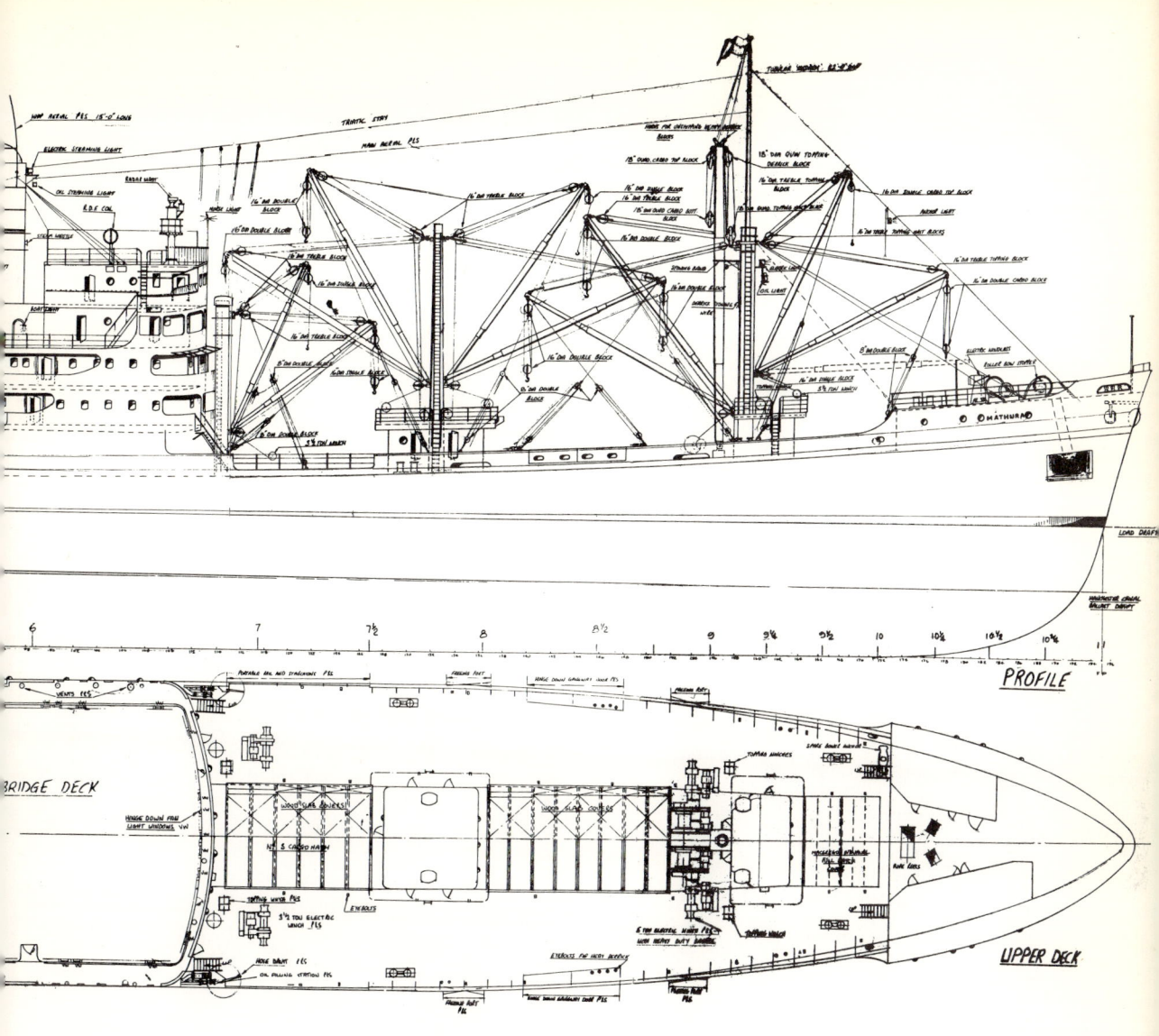

UPPER DECK

of deck providing access when large items of machinery had to be removed; normally, smaller items could be taken in or out by means of an overhead rail and a large door in the engine room casing, the rail being fitted with a chain hoist and led out on to the main deck.

A verandah deckhouse with large windows and open at the after end was provided at the after end of the boat deck, and usually a table tennis table was placed in there. A fixed swimming pool was installed at the after end of the centrecastle between

the two samson posts — a welcome feature on the tropical routes and an improvement on the canvas contraptions normally carried on similar ships in other companies.

The poop carried the normal deckhouse, with two other deckhouses, one port and one starboard, with wide open alleyways between. Another deckhouse was carried on the top of the poop deckhouse, with potato and vegetable lockers at the sides. A wooden awning was mounted at the fore end of the poop over the

warping winch. Two hawsepipes were fitted in the stern. This somewhat unusual feature was used when mooring in the River Hooghly off Calcutta during the bore tide season. These tides caused a large wave to pass down and return approximately twelve hours later each day, and when moored in the open roadstead it was necessary to unshackle sections of the anchor chain and drag them aft to moor up to special buoys in the river. Steam was kept on the main engines in case of accident, and standby watches

Left: the funnel, showing its shape and the fitting for the whip aerials. Note the shape of the square ventilator. This vessel, the *Masirah*, unlike the *Mathura*, had an engine room skylight.
Right: looking aft from the boat deck showing the cargo winches on the mast house, and the warping winch on the poop deck; note the extended warping drums on this winch.
(All uncredited photographs by the author).

were kept on the bridge and in the engine room for an hour or so at the time of the tides. The ship would often lift bodily a few feet as the wave passed under, and these hawsepipes could always be found on Brocklebank ships and British India ships normally spending a considerable period at Calcutta each voyage.

Ships in the company were normally well maintained, and the crew were kept chipping and painting for most of the homeward voyage. The colour scheme was very simple, usually black and white everywhere except for the blue band on the funnel and house flag. The crew ratings were almost exclusively

Indian or Pakistani, with occasional Maldivian ratings; many had served in the company all their lives and had survived wartime sinkings.

The *Mathura*, 497ft long overall, 63ft 5in moulded breadth, and 35ft deep, was of riveted and welded construction, a feature being the thick doubler riveted to the hull at the ends of the bridge deck amidships as a strengthener. The propelling machinery consisted of a set of Parsons-type steam turbines, HP and LP, driving a single screw through a set of double reduction gears, steam being provided by two Foster Wheeler watertube boilers at $800°F$ at superheater outlet and 610psi. An auxiliary donkey boiler

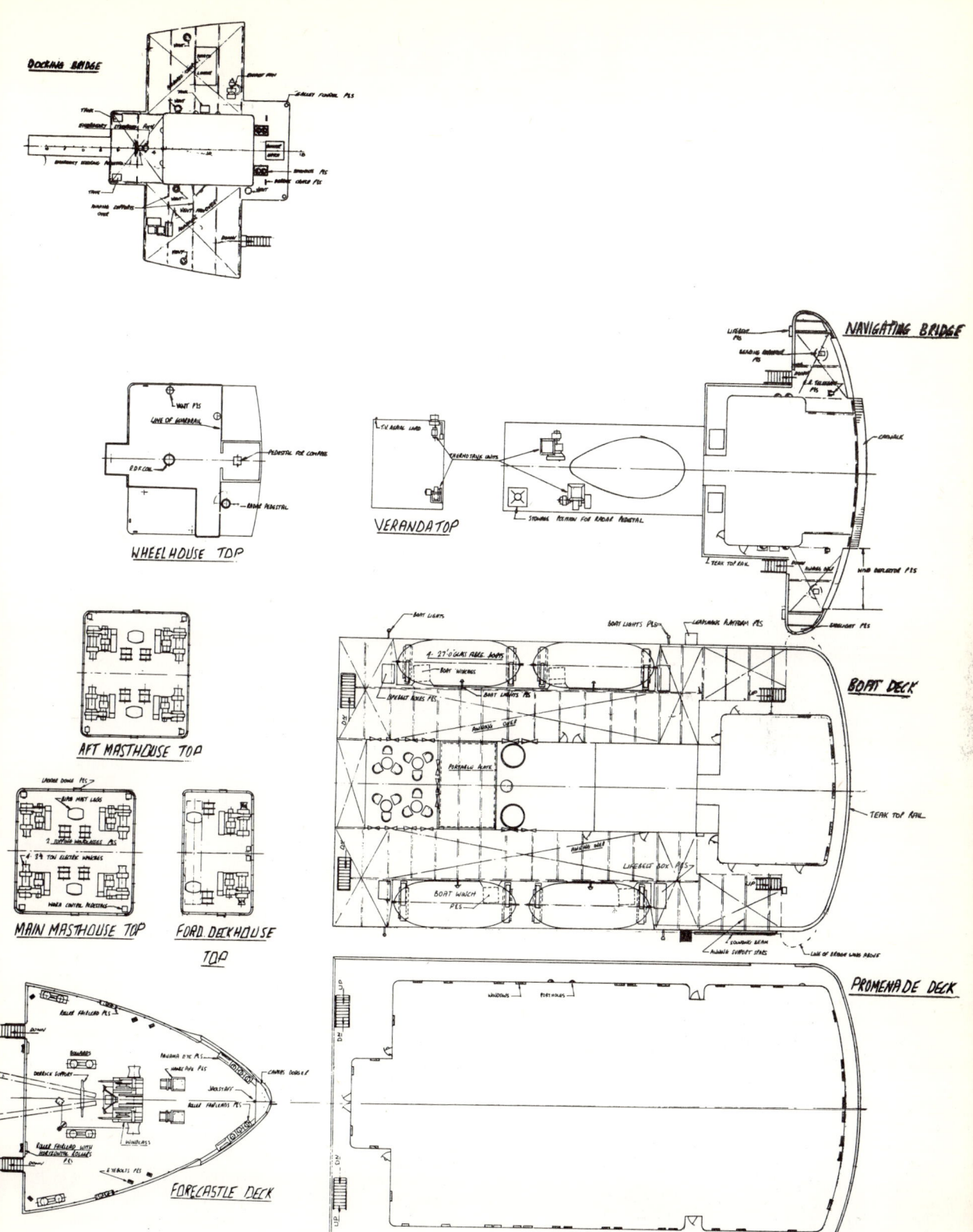

DOCKING BRIDGE

NAVIGATING BRIDGE

WHEELHOUSE TOP

VERANDA TOP

AFT MASTHOUSE TOP

MAIN MASTHOUSE TOP

FORD. DECKHOUSE TOP

BOAT DECK

PROMENADE DECK

FORECASTLE DECK

and steam generator supplied auxiliary steam at 120psi. The electrical requirements were met by four diesel-driven 352kw AC generators, current being 440volt 6h AC. At 8000shp the normal cruising speed was 15-16kts. The gross tonnage was 6125 tons.

The *Mathura* was sold out of the company in 1972 to the Compania Maritima San Baslia SA of New York, renamed *Eurytion* and registered in Piraeus. She was sold again in 1975 to Ta Chi Navigation (Panama) Corporation SA of Panama, retaining her name. Next she was sold in 1977 to Al Mouaket Shipping & Trading Co Ltd of Kuwait, renamed *Alwaha*, and was placed under the management of Common Bros (Management) Ltd of Newcastle-upon-Tyne. Finally she arrived off Karachi under tow on 29 October 1978, having been sold 'as damaged' to Pakistani shipbreakers.

ACKNOWLEDGEMENTS

I would like to thank Mr W Smart, chief draughtsman of Lithgow Ltd for providing drawings, Mr Peter White for information regarding eventual fate, and the Cunard Steamship Company for supplying the photograph of the ship under way and for checking the text.

PAINT SCHEME

Hull black with broad white band, boot topping red
Superstructure, deckhouses, ends of forecastle and poop, inside of bulwarks, masts and derricks, samson posts white
Boats and davits white, boat covers natural canvas (white)
Ventilators white, except those on engine casing which are black
Windlass, winches light grey
Forecastle deck, upper deck, bridge deck, top of mast houses, top of hospital, top of verandah black
Promenade deck and boat deck green composition
Navigating Bridge deck, poop deck, and top of wheelhouse wood deck
Underside of overhanging decks light green
Awnings white
Canvas covered sun deck white
Funnel black, with broad white and broad light blue bands

THE UNION JACK CODE

by Alec A Purves

Some six years ago, in answer to a query received (*Model Shipwright*, Vol 2 No 1 – Autumn 1973), I gave a brief explanation of the so-called 'Union Jack' Code. Since then several enquiries have been received about this 'mysterious' signal code, and since a representative hoist might well improve a model warship or merchant ship, it could perhaps prove both interesting and useful to go into the matter a little further. But first let me say that the name is slightly misleading, since the flag frequently employed in the code was not the Union Jack as such, but the British Pilot Jack – the Union Jack with the white border.

There were, in fact, two codes, or signal books, involved, the first being a pre-1914 publication, the *British Signal Manual,* and the second a wartime code based on the earlier one but enlarged and revised, the *Allied Signal Manual.* My copy of the first is dated 1912, and 'supersedes all former editions'. It certainly was in existence in 1905, as the *Admiralty Library Catalogue* for 1912 lists a copy dated 1905, and I would think that was probably the first edition. As regards the second version, while mine is dated January 1918, I believe I once had a copy dated 1917, but would think it had been in use for a few years before this. The *British Signal Manual* is stated to be 'for use between HM Ships and British Merchant Vessels, British Merchant Vessels and one another, and certain Signal Stations', but primarily for the first of these. The introduction mentions that the 'International Code Signal Book is in no way altered or interfered with', so we see the *British Signal Manual* as

supplementary to that code.

The book starts with flags having special significations. For example, a warship hoists a Red Ensign to communicate with a British merchant ship, and this was kept flying while making the signal. A Red Ensign over E (all letters and the Code Pendant refer to the International Code flags) indicated that the warship was willing to exercise signals (or was so doing) with a British merchant ship – a practice which was warmly encouraged by the Admiralty. The flag, E, hoisted by a British merchant ship showed that she wished, or was willing, to exercise signals with a British warship or merchant ship; this was hauled down when the exercise started, and re-hoisted when finished. The Code Pendant (CP) over *three* letters indicated a signal from the *British Signal Manual* (using ZOA to ZYX, which were not used in the International Code). A Red Ensign over J showed that a warship wished to communicate by semaphore; F at the yardarm of a warship indicated the ship having the Guard, and to which information or assistance (other than medical) requests should be made.

But the section of the manual which gave its unofficial name to the code is the Pilot Jack Table for reporting warships sighted. The use of the British Pilot Jack shows that this table is being used, and its position in the hoist shows the direction in which the ships were steering, thus: when 1st flag in the hoist, northward; 2nd flag, southward; 3rd flag, eastward; 4th flag, westward (if *two pendants,* indicating nationality, or *two flags,* representing numbers, appear above the Pilot Jack, they are to be regarded as one flag). Pendants show the nationality as follows: Code Pendant – unknown; C – Japanese; D – Russian; E – French; F – British; G – German; CD – USA; CE – Italian; CF – Austrian, etc. Flags (ie rectangular) in which red appears indicated numbers, 1 to 10 (or 0), being B, H, O, R, T, U, V, W, Y, Z, respectively. Flags without red indicated classes of warships, A, I, J, K, L, M, N, P, Q, S, X – large fleet, small fleet, battleships, large cruisers, small cruisers, armed merchant ships, submarines, torpedo boats or TBDs, transports with troops, fleet auxiliaries (including hospital and store ships), and colliers, respectively. Thus G, O, Pilot Jack, L, meant German, 3, steering to east, small cruisers. If necessary to add time or day (for which the ordinary International Code signals were used) or for mixed sightings, two or more hoists would be made. Thus if in addition to the three small German cruisers there was also a battleship, a second hoist, G, B, Jack, J, would have been hoisted.

The Special Table of Signals, ZOA to ZYX (not in the International Code Book, which stopped at ZNW) for items which might prove useful, was to be used with the Code Pendant above, in case the International Code were extended to include these letters. They were listed under the headings of Ordnance and Ammunition, Coal and Oil, &c, Convoy, Enemy, Hospital Ships, Torpedo, Water Distilling, Signalling, Miscellaneous, and Spare Signals. They include such signals as CP/ZOD – *What ammunition have you on board?;* CP/ZPC – *What is the length of your ship in feet?;* CP/ZRS – *The enemy has put to sea;* CP/ZVB – *Prepare to be taken in tow.*

The *Allied Signal Manual* basically fulfilled the same purpose as the earlier work, but extended it to both allied warships and allied (or neutral) merchant ships. By 1918 it had also been printed in Danish, French, Greek, Italian, Japanese, Portuguese and Spanish, but I have never seen any of these editions.

In addition to the flags of the International Code, pilot jacks and merchant ensigns of allied and neutral countries, the code used one special flag, the Mine Flag – white over blue, divided diagonally from top right to bottom left.

When the pilot jack or merchant ensign are referred to in the book, they mean those of the country to which the ship making the signal belonged, unless specially stated to the contrary.

Distinguishing signals were in use, for two purposes, namely to *speak* to any ship or convoy column, and to *indicate* any ship or column. For the columns of a convoy, UB to UM, over the Code Pendant, indicated columns 1 to 12, while the ships were distinguished by pilot jack over UL to YA, all representing double figures of which the first showed the column and the second the position of the ship in the column. Thus PJ/UW meant ship No 21, ie second column, first ship. If this signal were hoisted below the merchant ensign, it told the convoy that ship No 21 was to take the Guide of the Convoy. When a convoy met an escort, all ships had to hoist their distinguishing signals, while if a destroyer escort, they had in addition to display name boards.

The same Warship Sighting Table was used, but several other tables were added, such as True Compass Table, in degrees – AB/Pilot Jack, 0° (true north), to OJ/PJ, 359° (omitting all double letters, as the 1901 International Code had no substitute flags); thus, ED/Pilot Jack = 103° (S 77° E, true) and EF/PJ = 104° (S 76° E, true). The table of single flags, A to Y, included such items as F – *Am disabled; communicate with me,* or 0 – *Get into your correct station.*

In addition to the single letters, there were a few other special signals, such as a ship's Merchant Ensign flown at the main masthead, by the ship ordered to be the Guide of the Convoy temporarily (and as before, hoisted over a ship's distinguishing signal, it directed that ship to be the Guide); there was also the Mine Flag – *Mine in sight,* with the compass bearing added if necessary, and to be repeated by all ships; the Pilot Jack, as the sign of the leading ship of each column.

A single letter over the Code Pendant was a danger signal, and usually required instant action. These ran from A to X, plus the single letter, U (without Code Pendant) – *You are standing into danger.* Examples are J/Code Pendant – *Submarine or suspicious object in sight ahead,* V/CP – *Aircraft reported approaching, probably hostile.*

In addition to the single Mine Flag, already mentioned, there were a number of signals with the Mine Flag over a single letter, such as MF/E – *Have struck a mine,* MF/T – *Ships fitted with otter sweeps will lead down swept channel.* The Pilot Jack over a single letter, A to Z, gave a manoeuvring signal, such as PJ/G – *Resume your station on the beam of the Guide,* PJ/Q – *Cease zig-zagging, continue present course,* while below a single letter it was a positional, course, or speed signal, eg J/PJ – *Reduce speed quarter of a knot.*

The Special Signals, from ZOA to ZYX, were quite different from those in the 1912 *British Signal Manual,* the whole system having been revised to meet the war conditions; moreover, there is no mention of having to hoist the Code Pendant above the letters. Examples are: ZOG – *Prepare to anchor,* ZUB – *Kite balloon in sight,* ZXF – *Make as much smoke as possible to screen ships of convoy from submarine attack,* ZXR – *Have been struck by a torpedo.*

The two books contain much more information, though mainly routine signalling matters concerned with normal International Code practice, morse and semaphore signalling, etc. The 1912 *British Signal Manual* has iii + 76 pages, with coloured illustrations in the text, while the 1918 *Allied Signal Manual* has a slightly larger format, with iv + 111 pages and three coloured plates of signal flags, merchant ensigns and pilot jacks.

From the foregoing, there should be sufficient choice of suitable material for the model maker to find an unusual signal hoist for either a warship or a merchant vessel of the period (before and during the 1914-18 war – something that will perhaps puzzle the onlooker, but for which the maker will be able to produce an authenticated answer.

How I got under way

by Delmar Searle

I am an amateur model shipbuilder who is unable to spend a great deal of time on his hobby. I have absolutely no training in the manual arts. I do not have an elaborate workshop. In fact most of my work is done in the corner of a bedroom. I do have, however, a great interest in model ships and definite goals that I am actively pursuing. I am writing this article because I am sure that there are many others like me, and I hope that I can encourage some of those who are feeling frustrated at their progress (or apparent lack of it) and who may feel that their goals are out of reach. I suspect that more people give up ship-modeling as a hobby because of these frustrations than for any other reason. I trust that my ideas will encourage a few of you to dig out your tools and start to work.

GETTING STARTED
The hardest part of any new hobby is getting started. There are two aspects involved. One is physical preparation, which would include a workspace, tools, and materials. Many have written notes related to these areas and I will not repeat their advice here. Instead I will comment on the mental preparation, for in some respects it is more important than the physical. I believe that there are two common mistakes made by many beginners. The first is that they allow their initial enthusiasm to get out of control and as a result choose a project that is not suitable for their talents. The second is that they imagine that they will maintain this high degree of enthusiasm to such an extent that they will be willing to work hard and fast to finish that clipper ship in five or six weeks. What happens? First of all they find the work much harder than they expected. And not only is it harder, but some of it is downright boring! Consequently they begin to realize that their timetable was hopelessly over-optimistic and their enthusiasm wanes. At this point some just give up, feeling that ship-modeling is not for them.

What can be done to avoid this? First of all choose a model (probably a kit) that requires only basic skills and can be completed in a reasonable period of time. Secondly, prepare

yourself mentally to face the facts that (a) your ship will not be done as soon as you would like, (b) the work will be difficult and at times boring, and (c) your enthusiasm will wane and at times you will not feel like working on your model. With this kind of preparation you will not be unduly concerned when you find yourself becoming discouraged and you can take comfort in knowing that if you wait your enthusiasm will return.

THE FIRST MODEL

In retrospect I see that I probably made the first mistake, namely choosing a model a bit beyond my ability and knowledge. I chose a full kit model of the whaler *Charles W Morgan*. The kit came from the

Marine Model Co, Inc. and included a rough-carved hull, shaped spars, wood material, and metal fittings, as well as plans and instructions. While I did have some experience (ten years earlier as a child) with plastic models of sailing ships, my skills and knowledge were not fully adequate. I had, however, prepared myself for hard work, slow progress, and frustration. A full kit reduces the time required to complete a model by eliminating the need for constructing the small fittings and details. This is accomplished at the expense of realism and accuracy. Nevertheless it is a good choice for a beginner for it allows him to get acquainted with some basic woodworking skills, and some of the nomenclature associated with ships and their rigging. In my case I believe I managed to produce an attractive model and, in spite of its faults, am proud of my first effort.

As you work on that first model you will begin to dream of future models; all kinds of them. I

remember a phase when I purchased all kinds of published plans thinking that some day I would build each ship. Slowly I began to realize that I would never be able to build them all. My ultimate goal became the construction of an Admiralty-style model at $\frac{1}{4}$in = 1ft of a 74 gun two-decker. I had not yet finished my first full kit model and there I was dreaming of a model of a third rate ship-of-the-line. It was time to do some more mental preparation. I did not have the skills. I did not have the tools or the money to buy them. All I had was a dream.

TWO MORE

It was at that point that I established a plan of action. I decided to adopt a sequence of model construction that would allow me to develop my skills a little at a time to avoid a feeling of defeat at my clumsiness and ignorance, and that would also allow me time to build a modest inventory of tools. The plan involved three

additional models: a hull kit model, a scratch-built model using the bread and-butter or lift technique, and a scratch-built plank-on-frame model.

My second model was the *Mayflower*, built from a hull kit from Model Shipways, Inc The hull kit included a rough-carved hull, shaped spars, wood material. plans, instructions, but no metal fittings. Not only did I increase my range of skills by doing more actual construction, I also refined my techniques on those tasks I had already learned.

The next model was my first scratch-built model: a Great Lakes schooner *Challenge* built about 1850 It was built from plans supplied by A J Fisher, Inc. You may have noticed that as I built models requiring more and more work done by hand I also chose models of less complicated ships. I did not want to discourage myself by being over ambitious.

A PROBLEM
Up to the completion of this third model my plan was a success. I had learned a great deal and perhaps more importantly was beginning to see just how much I still did not know. However, I found myself extremely discouraged after the *Challenge* was completed. There were several reasons for this.

For one thing I needed some relatively expensive tools and did not know if I could afford to spend that much money. Also, I did not know any other person who was interested in building model ships. As a result I felt sort of lonely with respect to my hobby. Sure I read books and periodicals, but I had no one to talk to or share with, even in writing. Lastly, the step from a lift model to a plank-on-frame model seemed gigantic, indeed impossible. There were so many things I did not know how to do. And along this line one of the things I found most discouraging was, believe it or not, articles written in journals like *Model Shipwright*. Why? The answer is simple. Most of the articles were written by accomplished modelers, or professionals. Occasionally an article would be written by a 'beginner' but even then the author usually had an extensive background in the manual arts or some related field. Also very few articles were written for the modeler who is beyond the beginner stage, but not yet accomplished. Consequently most articles pass over certain tasks with the implied assumption that you should already know how to do it.

For example, how many authors tell you *how* to turn a cannon on a lathe? I have a fairly good library of books and periodicals dealing with ship-modeling techniques and even the most widely known authorities are of no real help. Let us look at the situation assuming that you have a lathe and at least some rudimentary instruction concerning its use. The problem is to turn a number of identical cannon barrels. Longridge in his *Anatomy of Nelson's Ships* comments that 'it is a fairly simple matter for an amateur to turn out one of these guns on a lathe; but it is quite another matter when it comes to turning out several dozen all exactly the same'. He goes on to describe how he had a contour tool manufactured at a local engineering works.

Petrejus in *Modeling the Brig-of-War 'Irene'* simply advises us to cut yourself a steel template, shaped to the profile of the gun, to check the taper and finish the many rings of the barrel'. He also comments on casting barrels. To one who has no idea of where to start these suggestions mean little. It is not my intent to demean these gentlemen. I thoroughly enjoy their books and have found a great deal of useful information in them. My point simply is that at that time I could not find the information I needed to progress. The written material was either too elementary, or else assumed too much.

THE SOLUTION
I was faced then with three problems. Two events led to the solution. The first event was the purchase of a Unimat lathe with the table saw attachment. While it is simple to state, it was not an easy decision. I have not regretted it.

The second event was my becoming acquainted with a professional modeler. It would be difficult to overestimate the

Opposite: the Mayflower came next - again a kit model, but one from which I learned a lot.
Above: my third model, the *Challenge*, which proved to be an ideal subject for a first scratch-built model.
Right: some of the detail incorporated in the *Challenge*.

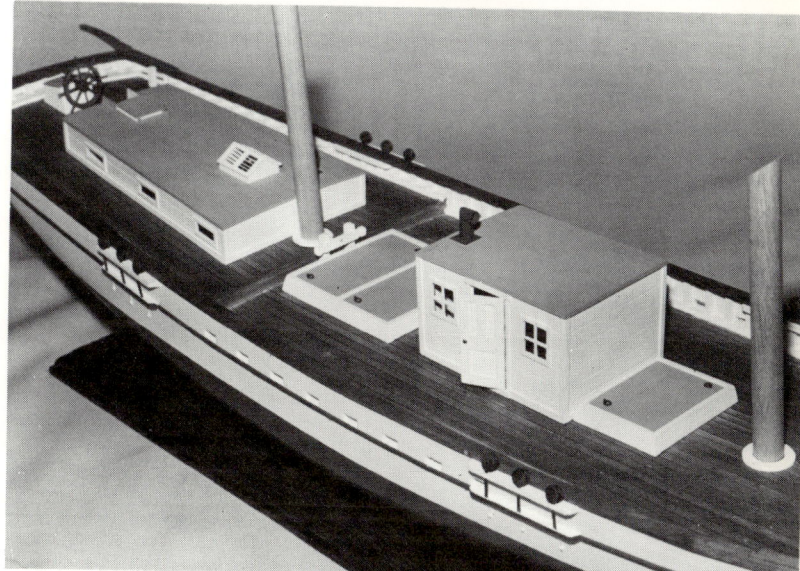

contribution he has made with regard to my model building activity. I had been particularly fascinated by a couple of models at a national museum and made a mental note of the builder's name as listed on the description plate in the display case. A short time later I saw the same name in a journal related to ships and noticed that he lived in the town where I was born. Not knowing if this was the same man nor how he would respond, I hesitated to write. But finally I did. As it turned out it was the same man, and his response was most gracious. I am greatly indebted to him for his kindness and willingness to assist me. Even though we live nine hundred miles apart and have only seen each other twice he provided the moral support and the guidance that I needed to take the leap and start a plank-on-frame model.

On his advice, I chose as my subject the row-galley *Washington* used by the Americans on Lake Champlain and captured by the British in October of 1776. The lines plan was obtained from the National Maritime Museum in London, and an additional plan was obtained from the Smithsonian Institute in Washington DC. The hull is simple

and in fact virtually the entire middle third of the hull has exactly the same shape, reducing the amount of work involved in completing the framing. This model (as well as the *Challenge*) was left unrigged due to lack of adequate storage space. I found, as I am sure many others before me have found, that it was not nearly as difficult as I had imagined. But without the help of an experienced modeler I would never have completed the model; I probably would not have even started it!

THE FUTURE
My goal has not changed. I still plan to build a 74-gun two-decker, but

first to build a brig, then a larger ship of around 20 guns, then a 50-gun two-decker, and finally the 74. After that who knows? The point is that I am continuing my plan of building so that I have time to develop my skills slowly and carefully and when I do build the 74, I'll do it right.

CONCLUSIONS
I firmly believe that new or relatively inexperienced modelers will be far more likely to succeed if the following suggestions are adopted.

1. Make adequate mental preparation. Adopt a plan of construction that will allow you to progress slowly. Recognize that you

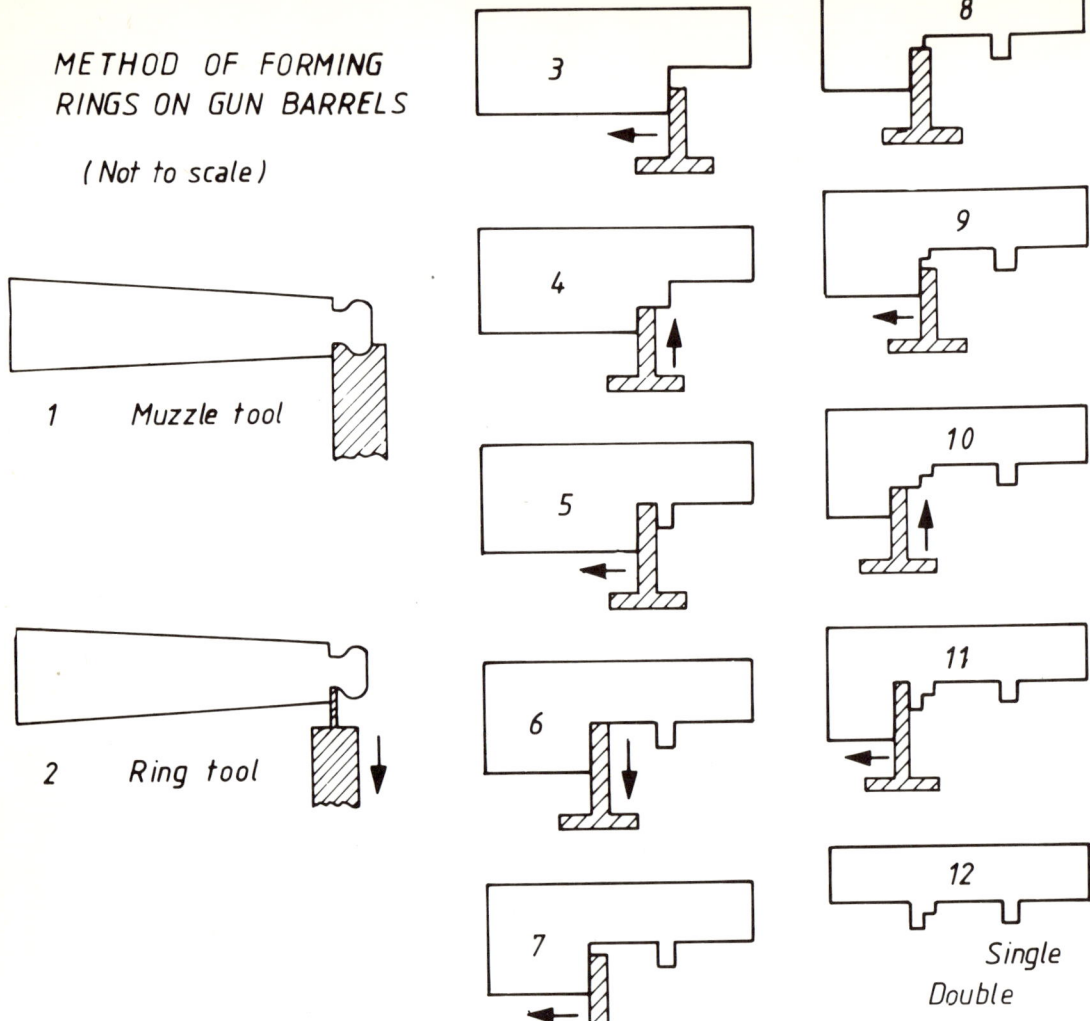

METHOD OF FORMING RINGS ON GUN BARRELS

(Not to scale)

1 Muzzle tool

2 Ring tool

3

4

5

6

7

8

9

10

11

12

Single
Double

may not enjoy all of the tasks involved, and that you will not always feel like working on your model. Keep in mind that you may take two years or longer to finish a model.

2. Find a friend. If you do not know anyone, write to strangers. You could write to authors of articles, members of model clubs, or maybe even editors of ship-modeling periodicals. Maybe the person you write to cannot help but he might know someone who can! Somewhere you will find someone who can and will help you. But do not forget that your new friend is busy. I made it a point not to write more frequently than once a month.

3. Purchase tools when you need them. I realize that it is easy to say, but not always easy to do. Be willing to save money wherever you can in order to buy your tools. You'll be glad you did.

4. Be patient!

TURNING CANNON

I cannot finish without a last comment on turning cannon. How do I do it? Unlike most people I choose to use aluminium; is a soft metal, light, and inexpensive. First, grind a tool-bit for the shape of the muzzle and another for the shape of the inboard (or breech) end. Set the headstock at a slight angle to produce the taper. You will have to experiment to find the correct

setting. Next turn the round stock until the muzzle end will fit inside an appropriate sized hole·in a drill gauge. By slightly rotating the gauge a mark is left on the stock where the barrel actually contacts the gauge material. This is the widest point of the bell. The muzzle tool is advanced using the vertical feed until the widest portion of the bell barely makes contact with the tool. The inboard edge of the tool cuts the outer shoulder of the first reinforcing ring at the same time. The muzzle tool is replaced by a tool ground to a thin projection with a virtually flat end. The inboard shoulder of the tool is started against the outer shoulder of the first ring with the tip against the body of the

46

Top: this scratch-built model of the row galley *Washington* followed the *Challenge*. Notice the long parallel mid-body of the hull, which considerably eased the constructional work.
Centre: some of the deck detail on the *Washington* - Navy Board style. The guns were made by the method referred to in the article.
Bottom: the bluff bow of the *Washington* called for some careful and intricate plank work!
All photographs by the author

barrel. Using the vertical feed the tool is withdrawn a distance equal to the thickness of the ring. Using the horizontal feed the tool is moved inboard a distance corresponding to the width of the ring plus the width of the cutting portion of the tool. Using the vertical feed again the tool is moved back into its original position completing the first reinforcing ring. Using the horizontal feed the tool is moved to the position of the second ring and the process is repeated. Double bands are produced by a second withdrawal prior to returning the tool to its original position using the vertical feed. When the reinforcing rings are completed the breech tool is used. The completed barrel is cut off using a razor saw, and a little filing cleans up the cut.

After reading the available literature, I found this technique refreshingly simple. The turning is reduced to a series of numbers indicating the proper operation of the feed screws and produces a series of barrels that are virtually identical. Did I figure this out by myself? No — my friend did.

A CARAVEL/DHOW CONNECTION

by Grahame Wilson

A look into intriguing similarities between a European ship of the fifteenth century and some Arab vessels afloat today

Is it possible to step back nearly five centuries into time and arrive again in a period of mediaeval ships? A good question and one I asked myself. Was there a definite link between a twentieth century Red Sea sambuk, for example, and a Portuguese caravel of the fifteenth century at the time of Prince Henry the Navigator? It was a challenge that could not be ignored, and significantly, a tantalizing one.

To my knowledge, research of this kind has not been done before, but whether any connection could be proved convincingly today is open to doubt. Bjorn Landstrom in his beautifully illustrated book *The Ship* (surely well known to readers for the unsurpassed quality of the author's drawings) raises the question briefly that a sambuk in particular, or the baggala in general, may be direct descendants of Henry's caravels. Landstrom does not elaborate. However, before World War II there were still some 40 or so of the old baggalas afloat to study. Today one would not find many Arab vessels of any type in Arab waters, and none at all is in commission without some kind of modern engine power. The days of the dhow are clearly numbered.

IS THERE A CONNECTION?
The most obvious and interesting question is that both Moslem and Christian vessels use the triangular lateen sail. There are differences, of course, which if space permits we can look into later. But the importance and significance of the lateen rig cannot be underestimated and are best summed up in the words of that well known yachtsman Douglas Phillips-Birt. He wrote: 'The lateen rig has perhaps the most prominent place amongst all the rigs used to propel ships; and one of great significance too in the history of man, a little less than the plough or the wheel, but greater than the galleon, the stage coach, or those suits of armour on which the knightly system of chivalry depended.' Quite some statement!

The lateen, we believe, originated as an Arab rig as early as the

Opposite: a caravel at the time of Prince Henry the Navigator, as depicted in the National Maritime Museum, Lisbon: a frail but intrepid vessel which, by using new techniques, enabled men for the first time to navigate far from land in any weather. *(Photograph by permission of the Museu de Marinha, Lisbon).*

Top: a 2-masted caravel under sail, after a drawing on an early Portuguese map by Simao Bening. It is from rather indifferent pictures such as this that authorities have had to try and reconstruct what the caravels of old may have looked like.

Bottom: a typical ocean-going dhow. The lateen sails are not fully triangular as are a caravel's, but quadrilateral. The 4-cornered lateen is general amongst most Arab ocean-going vessels.

thirteenth century and reached Portugal via the Mediterranean. Lateen sails were especially manageable in changing winds but it was the Western Europeans, notably the Portuguese, who were the inspired adaptors, even improvers of this Eastern inheritance. To whom posterity owes this unique invention no one can tell, but there is every indication that at Sagres, Portugal, Prince Henry developed a revolutionary ocean-going vessel from early Mediterranean fishing boats with lateen sails, first with two masts, then with three. The hypothesis, then, is that in sending these vessels south along Africa in exploration of a sea-route to the east, the caravel (as Portuguese ships with the lateen were now known) may have gone full circle — back via the Cape of Good Hope this time — and that one of Henry's ships might have survived to this century in the embodiment of an Arab vessel long after the European vessel died out. An interesting speculation.

No archaeological finds of mediaeval ships have been made that can even remotely be compared with the Gokstad and Oseberg Viking ships some four centuries earlier. Alas, the problems of marine archaeology of the fifteenth century, as we all know, are greatly accentuated by the almost complete lack of contemporary evidence, both documentary and pictorial. Few illustrations of a caravel exist, and those that do are difficult to interpret. To judge how difficult this is one just has to look at the two illustrations reproduced with

this article, which are taken from maps of the period. However, if we look at these illustrations the first thing that strikes us is that the caravel was a vessel of light and rakish appearance, low in the water and with the minimum amount of draught. Early versions were little better than open boats with no sleeping quarters provided save perhaps for the master and pilot. Ordinary seamen slept on or below deck, or wherever they could find room. Later types appeared to have a short forecastle over the bow, but as in all caravels the fore superstructure would have been kept to a minimum because of the unique workings of the lateen rig — anything too large would be an obstruction in the way of the long yardarm of the sail. Thus the little evidence that remains presents us with a challenge. But in so saying it can also give scope to that kind of history seeker who, presented with 'no facts' will endeavour to make those facts a kind of historical *fait accompli*. I would not like to fall into this trap.

THE IMPORTANCE OF THE CARAVEL

It appeared to me that the most reasonable solution in writing about a caravel/dhow connection was to present certain information and ask readers of *Model Shipwright* to draw their own conclusions. The importance of the caravel to us cannot be underestimated. The caravel was to the fifteenth century what the Apollo/Saturn project is to the twentieth. The parallel is obvious. The introduction of this type of ship was 'one giant leap for mankind' in the fifteenth century. It was the vessel on which Renaissance man spread the wings of his imagination and which extended his vision far beyond the horizon. It took us beyond the barriers of fear, of sea-monsters, and where the boiling sea destroyed all who were not already scorched black by the heat of the noonday sun. It took us to the southern half of the globe — another hemisphere. For the first time since the Vikings man was venturing safely out of sight of home shores. He could ride out the gales of the southern Atlantic or, if he wished, just as easily slip into some

estuary and navigate upstream on unknown rivers into the very heart of unexplored territory. In other words the caravel was the perfect vessel for exploration — tailor made for the day, as it were. It took a special type of seaman and a special type of boat (under Diogo Cao, for example) to pass through a section of the river Congo, known as Hell's Cauldron, where the current surges through a narrow passage of whirlpools at 10kts — an amazing feat of seamanship, akin to Armstrong navigating *Eagle* down on to the Sea of Tranquillity.

However, the story of the caravel is a contradiction of time and place. Its rise to fame appears to be as rapid as its demise. 'The glory' ended with Bartholomeo Dias in 1488, the first European to round the southern tip of Africa and point the way to the East. Dias returned to Portugal with his caravels after a gruelling sixteen and a half months at sea, a voyage fraught with deprivations, scurvy, storms, and eventually the threat of mutiny which turned him back. Dias had just taken his ships through an area notorious the world over for its high seas and dangerous coastline. Back in Portugal however, he not surprisingly urged Da Gama (who was to follow next) to build not caravels but square-rigged vessels, with higher freeboard the better to withstand the gales of the southern Atlantic and which could carry more stores — advice which the irascible Vasco da Gama wisely heeded. What is interesting here is that in pinpointing the way to India Dias had just made the caravel obsolete.

The 'glory of the caravel' had lasted a mere fifty years, from about 1440 (for Azurara states that at that time caravels were used by Henry's captains) to 1488 and the Cape of Storms. Henry had already been dead for 28 years. There is evidence to suggest that about this time a 'hybrid' caravel was making an appearance. It was a vessel with up to four masts, lateen-rigged on three and with one foremast carrying a square foresail and fore topsail: a compromise, of course — a vessel trying to meet the new challanges of distance, space, cargo and more

stores. Like all hybrids it was neither the one nor the other ship. When it came to exploiting the riches of the new world it was the large gun-carrying, square-rigged galleons that won hands down every time. After all, commerce and exploitation was what it was all about.

Therefore, in looking at the above dates one sees immediately that the caravel era belongs approximately to the middle and second half of the fifteenth century — and not after it. It also belongs to the Atlantic west coast of Africa, and not the east (where the lateen-rigged dhow is found today) — symbolically stopping where that great dividing mass of land separates east from west, and where two great oceans meet.

WAS KIPLING WRONG?

We have understood that the quest for India was foremost a commercial affair, backed by speculators and carried out by adventurers. Religion was just a pretext. If the name of the day had just become big profit had the age of the 'true', or little, caravel surely gone?

It is at this point that we must pause and look at the 'other side'. From Suez south along the east African coast, east to the Persian Gulf and the west coast of India, Arabs, Persians and Indians have all used those graceful ocean-going lateeners which we — not they — call dhows*. Whether this has always been so, and where the dhow got its distinctive hull and sail, is still anybody's guess. In a moment we will look at a few possibilities, but let us consider first that 700 years before the Portuguese arrival these nationalities had been closely linked — politically, culturally and economically — with a sea-trading network that criss-crossed the seas as far as China. In other words the European 'discovery' of the Indian Ocean was only 'new' to the European. But within fifteen years of the Portuguese arrival this network was systematically smashed, and the largely unarmed Moslem shipping was swept from the sea — or, more appropriately, sent to the bottom of it.

What took their place in the void that followed? One of the problems facing the research worker is that the Arabs have not recorded their maritime history. They were great mariners, but their voyages have been unchronicled over centuries. Alan Villiers tells us that dhows are put together on the beaches of Sur and built by eye by carpenters who cannot follow the most elementary plan, the knowledge of the shipwrights having been passed down amongst themselves over generations. If Kipling is wrong, and the twain did meet, the flat-sterned dhow is as clear an example as anyone could ask for of a marriage of the traditional east with that of western shipbuilding. In the evolution of hull shapes the west have been the masters, and the east the pupils. John Jewell, author of *Dhows at Mombasa*, feels that most authorities today would hold that the sambuk is the result of alterations in the stern of a double-ended ship — a direct consequence of the arrival of the Portuguese. This is as far as the speculation goes for most. Any further 'westernization', other than nailed planks (which replaced traditional coir rope and pegs of Moslem shipping), would always remain the subject of the keenest controversy. There are many who point out the 'European-ness' of the carvings of the stern of the baggala, for example. They are of interest, but little else: Henry's ships are not to be found here. The broad, high transoms and quarter galleries, rich in carved embellishments, have almost certainly been copied line for line from European frigates and merchantmen of the eighteenth century. Where are Henry's caravels? If the ships of the fifteenth century were decorated it was with paintwork and not with the carvings and gilding of a later period. The smaller sambuks of the Red Sea often have decorations, gay with bands of paint and geometrical designs: blue, red, and green crescents, moons, stars and triangles. Even diamonds, hearts, spades and clubs are not unknown! This ardour for painting can even extend to fake windows with painted half-drawn curtains.

*Dhow is the generic English term for all Arab vessels: it is derived from the Swahili word signifying any small to medium-sized craft).

However, the caravel was surely a functional vessel, often fitted out and sponsored by business men, and it had to pay its way. The main adornment was likely to have been only the banner of Christ, a red cross emblazoned on the sails.

Alan Villiers writes that the big deep-sea dhows from Kuwait and Sur and the Persian ports are almost pure survival from the Phoenician days (see *Sons of Sinbad,* Hodder & Stoughton, p4). Villiers' influence is felt in the book *Dhows* by David Howarth, who talks a lot about ancient history. However, Professor Lionel Casson, in his *Illustrated History of Ships and Boats* (1964), thinks the baggala is comparatively new, its birth as recent as 1675 or thereabouts, and was introduced by none other than the British East India shipyards in Bombay, when Persian shipwrights working for the British were allowed to indulge their whim! Here we have as clear a picture

A 3-masted caravel after a drawing on a Portuguese map of 1520 by Lopo Homen. Note the large triangular lateen

as any of the many differences of opinion. Casson also believes the sambuk preceded the baggala by a century or so, which brings this vessel right into Portuguese influence of the early sixteenth century!

SAMBUK AND CARAVEL COMPARED

Let us now compare the sambuk — once the most common of Arab 'coasters' — with what we know of the caravel. Unfortunately, the only caravel we can refer to for any estimation of size is the famous *Nina* (albeit Spanish). She was one of two that sailed with the square-rigged *Santa Maria,* but it is said that Columbus preferred her to his own flagship. Admiral Morrison puts *Nina's* size at approximately 70ft (length) x 25ft (beam) x 6ft (draught), the dimensions being based on her known 60-tons burden. In those days a ton had a different meaning. It was

the measure of the number of 'tuns' of wine a ship could carry, a tun being about 40 cu ft. In comparison the Arabs do not measure their ships by tons, but by the stowage capacities of packages of dates. John Jewell in *Dhows at Mombasa* gives the average size of a sambuk as 80ft x 20ft x 10ft; displacement varies from 75 to 140 tons. A crew complement of 12 to 15 men can man a vessel of this size. *Nina* sailed to the Americas with a crew of 24, although this did not mean that all hands were needed to sail the ship.

The caravel has a record of sea-kindliness and ease of handling, and it is worthwhile giving two examples of this. Five crew members have been able to pilot a caravel on the open sea for two months without sighting land, as in the ill-fated Nuno Tristao expedition of 1446. The second example is the indomitable Alvise da Cadamosta. In 1456 this intrepid captain took

his caravels up the River Gambia a full 60 miles from the open sea. This would mean tacking against the river current in shifting wind patterns. The hazards of such ventures can be imagined: unexplored territory beset by hostile tribesmen, floating trees, submerged rocks and sandbanks, not to mention the hippopotamuses and elephants which the Portuguese were seeing for the very first time.

It is here that we must look at the very important lateen sail, which Phillips-Birt has already described for us as of great significance in the history of man. The characteristic feature of the lateen is its distinctive triangular shape, a three-cornered sail hung from a long tapered yard, suspended at an angle of approximately 45° from near the top of the mast. Only the European version is three-cornered however; the Arab version is quadrilateral. This rig is essentially the same as the

Mediterranean type except it looks as if someone has taken a large pair of scissors and snipped off a piece of the canvas at the lower forecorner of the sail leaving a short vertical luff. Just why this is so, and just why there is this difference between the two has never been satisfactorily explained to me. Perhaps a reader knows the answer? However, the great advantage of the lateen is that a vessel can be sailed close to the eye of the wind, very much like a modern yacht. This must have been truly revolutionary in Henry's time when early square-rigged ships never permitted an angle closer to the wind than 80°. But there is a saying amongst dhow seamen, 'nobody but a madman or a Christian would sail to windward', which may give an indication that the lateen also has its problems and why it has sometimes been described as the most dangerous rig man ever invented. Certainly it requires great

skill to control it properly. However, it was not the lateen that caused the caravel's demise, but the size of ship a lateen could drive and which could still pay its way on a far-flung sea-borne Empire. In the end it was left to the large, heavily-armed, square-rigged galleons to smash armadas and build Empires, not to the caravel.

Dhows today are nailed, but their predecessors hark back to those light boats which were sewn together with coir rope and were wholly devoid of iron in their construction. This would have limited the size of vessel that could be safely built for use in heavy seas. We Westerners often cite this as an example that sewn craft would not have proved seaworthy enough for voyages of exploration as European ships were. The caravel is reputed to have been built in the ratio of one to three (ie, the length was three times that of the beam) or even one to four.

This was revolutionary for a period when ships were generally broad and tubby, with beams sometimes equalling half their length — a one to two ratio. The caravel also had a flat stern and rudder — another revolutionary feature for the Middle Ages — and appears to have had a wider beam than say, a sambuk, with flaring sides. A sambuk is generally more 'up-and-down' from waterline to gunwale and sits deeper in the water. Below the waterline, the bow of a sambuk curves sharply back to the keel, although whether this is characteristic of all vessels I'm not certain. The caravel, on the other hand, was likely to have had a bow that was an arching curve from waterline to keel, in keeping with ships of her period. Above the waterline, both ships show marked similarities, especially if taken in silhouette. The sambuk and the baggala have stemposts of some kind, whether it is scimitar-shaped as in

some models of the sambuk, or comma-shaped as in the Indian kotias, and bear a strong resemblance to Portuguese vessels. The mainmast of the ocean-going dhow has a distinctive forward rake. This is to facilitate the swing of the yard from one side of the mast to the other. In the caravel this forward rake is not so apparent and suggests a difference in sail handling. Once again a reader may be able to comment on this?

CONCLUSIONS

To sum up, let us go back to the void that followed after the Portuguese arrival in the east decimated Moslem shipping. The backbone of the Portuguese fleet from 1500 onwards was the large, gun carrying square-rigged sailing ship, the armament of which was so totally unexpected and new in the Indian Ocean. At the height of Portugal's maritime power, about 1536, C R Boxer tells us she had no more than 300 ocean-going vessels. 'Impressive for a small country', he writes, 'but totally inadequate for a far-flung sea-borne Empire.' Portugal had the sole monopoly of supplying an insatiable Europe with the riches of the east. But what was needed to do this was to have whole fleets of ships — far more than one small country the size of Portugal could supply. Even if she had them, she did not have the manpower or resources to keep these ships at sea.

This problem was partly solved in two ways. One was the discovery and availability in India of that excellent shipbuilding material — teak. The manpower problem (ironically) was overcome by using the services of the vanquished. As early as the time of Alfonso de Albuquerque (1509-15) Portuguese ships were manned by Asian seamen working under white officers and gunners. Thus with the main Portuguese dockyard established at Goa we have a clear pattern forming; this was the birth of a European shipbuilding industry in the east, and the training of the local populace as seamen to man these vessels.

Monster galleons were built in the east for the spice run — the whole object of the shipbuilding exercise. Little recorded, however, is that the first vessels to be built were small boats for coastal duties, right down to fishing boats such as the frigata. All were vessels that could easily be replaced if lost, but it goes without saying that a fast and seaworthy coaster type would have been needed to take messages and supplies between the newly seized ports. Areas of the Persian Gulf, for example, are shallow and shoal infested, and without doubt the finest coaster of them all for waters such as these was the original small caravel with a draught of less than 6ft. More research has to be done to prove this, but for the moment there are some who feel it is logical to assume that it was so. Voyages of dhows today still consist largely of coastal trading and some smuggling; in earlier times it was piracy and slaving, something that Henry's caravels had been infamous for in north and west Africa.

The amount of space available in *Model Shipwright* precludes further detail. However, I would be interested to hear from anyone who has studied the subject, and indeed anyone who has tackled either a two-masted or three-masted caravel apropos Prince Henry's period. The intricacies of the rigging of a European lateen would be of interest, as would be the theory of sail handing adopted by those intrepid Portuguese navigators. My address is: 11 Oberon Way, Meadowridge, Cape Town 7800, South Africa.

Lastly, is there a caravel/dhow connection? The answer to this at the moment will always remind me of the Soviet aero-engineer when asked if the Tupolev Tu-144 supersonic transport owed any of its genealogy to the Anglo/French Concorde? 'Of course not', came the retort. 'They just happen to look the same, that's all.'

BIBLIOGRAPHY

Portuguese Seaborne Empire 1415-1825 C R Boxer
The Persian Gulf Sir Arnold Wilson
Sons of Sinbad Alan Villiers
The Dhow Clifford Hawkins
Dhows David Howarth
Dhows at Mombasa John H A Jewell
The Ship Bjorn Landstrom
The Quest for India Bjorn Landstrom
From the Congo to the Cape Professor Eric Axleson.

THE

In the intriguing and stimulating study of the shipwright's craft, things I have taken for granted — never thought much about, in fact — have a habit of assuming a new dimension, often totally unrelated to my first casual impression, when a chance remark or thought prompts a particular line of enquiry. This was again demonstrated to me when I began to think about the rake of the sternpost and its influence on the tiller and ultimately, the wheel. In almost all draughts which I have studied of seventeenth and eighteenth century vessels, those steered by whipstaff or wheel, as differentiated from a hand-held tiller, show sternposts raking between five and ten degrees. I began searching for an explanation and, being unable to find one, I can only present my own hypothesis for what it is worth and would welcome readers' comments.

As the tillers were long and heavy, (in *Crocodile*, 6th Rate, 1781, the tiller is 19ft in length and about 8in square) they required support at their forward end. Now, if the rudder post were vertical, ie if there were no rake to the sternpost, when the helm was put hard over the tiller would describe an arc in the horizontal plane so that the support, or 'sweep' or 'quadrant', would need to be horizontal likewise.

Headroom between decks was limited and this would impose a further restriction, as the tiller, when amidships, would be some 7 or 8in below the round-up of the deck beam above. This inconvenience was immediately alleviated when the

SHIP'S WHEEL

by K M Hobbs

sternpost was raked aft as the tiller would then describe an arc in the vertical plane as well as the horizontal and so follow the round-up or camber of the beam (see drawings). No doubt this was only one of a number of factors considered desirable for this rake aft, but it is of particular interest when considering the development of the wheel.

Well it might be wondered why the wheel was so long in appearing, and so superseding the whipstaff, particularly as the latter gave a very limited amount of rudder angle (4°

or 5°). However, a ship was sailed by the wind and this governed the course she made good so that a small amount of rudder angle was all that was normally required. After all, a modern yacht is controlled in a similar manner. If too much helm is needed then either the sails need trimming, the rake of the mast altered or even repositioned in extreme cases so as to adjust the sails' centre of effort as rudder angle retards speed. For manoeuvering, the spritsails played an important part. William Richardson in *A Mariner of England* refers to 'steering sails' being set when running before the wind.

Probably a prime factor in the long retention of the whipstaff were the leads of the tiller-ropes and the mechanical problem of taking up the slack in the rope as the helm was put hard over. To some extent this could be lessened by the positioning of the lead blocks, but it was not until the mid-eighteenth century that the idea of utilising the supporting sweep was adapted and the problem overcome.

In discussing the steering it is interesting to look at the rudder. The height of the lower hance was approximately at the level of the load waterline and the fore and aft breadth of the rudder was much reduced

FIGURE 1
(a) End elevation of wheel support
(b) Method of securing the spokes with rims and hubs each side
(c) Side view of drum or barrel and wheel

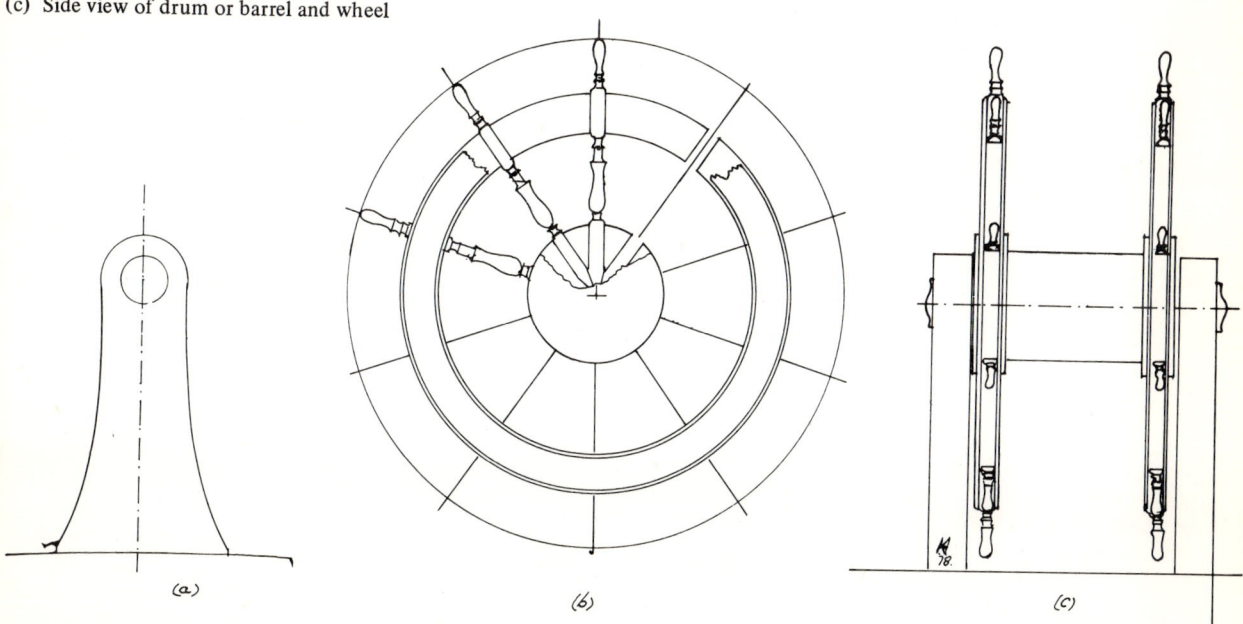

(a)   (b)   (c)

above this. The purpose was to reduce the shock from heavy seas and the gradual reduction in fore and aft breadth from the keel up was to help compensate for the greater angle of incidence due to the fuller body of the ship near the waterline. In spite of these measures, the wheel could still give a mighty 'kick' and would need extra men and relieving tackles to control it in bad weather.

Two wheels were also standard practice in larger ships.

METHOD OF CONSTRUCTION

The draught showed the diameter of the wheels and drum. From this I drew the wheel and supports as shown, on a scale 1in = 1ft (figure 1). From a piece of box — any well-seasoned fine grained wood would be suitable — I turned the rim of the

wheel and boss, as shown in figure 2. I then parted this off but left the boss section attached to the rim. On a piece of drawing paper I then marked off the exact positions of the spokes. By dividing a large circle it was easier to space them evenly.

Next, I lightly glued this turned piece on to the drawing which I had already glued to a scrap of wood, being careful to make the centres

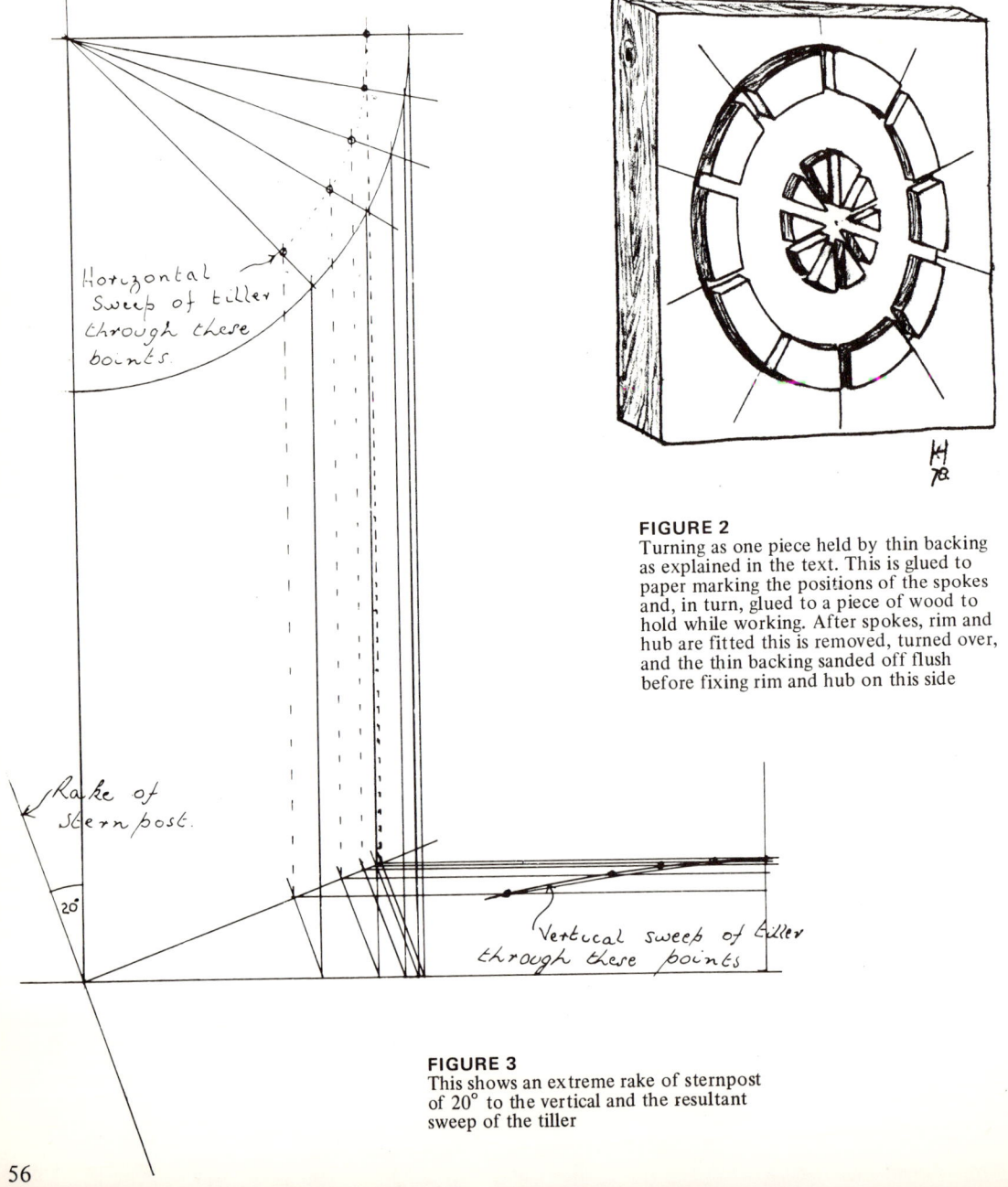

FIGURE 2
Turning as one piece held by thin backing as explained in the text. This is glued to paper marking the positions of the spokes and, in turn, glued to a piece of wood to hold while working. After spokes, rim and hub are fitted this is removed, turned over, and the thin backing sanded off flush before fixing rim and hub on this side

Horizontal sweep of tiller through these points.

Rake of sternpost.

20°

Vertical sweep of tiller through these points

FIGURE 3
This shows an extreme rake of sternpost of 20° to the vertical and the resultant sweep of the tiller

coincide. With a jeweller's saw, I cut down each division, followed this with a knife-edged file and finally squared off the mortices with a sharp chisel (figure 2). From a piece of applewood — which I have discovered turns better than box — I turned the spokes. I found that by beginning at the outer end and turning from a firm piece held in the chuck, I had no trouble or breakages.

A template showed the sections to be shaped. Those parts required to be square and tenon into the mortices I turned slightly oversize and later squared up with a chisel and then a square drawplate. The spokes were put into place, as illustrated in figure 1b.

The next step was to turn up two rims and hubs. I cut these off on the lathe with a fine jeweller's saw,

rotating the lathe by hand as I did so. I glued them face down on a piece of newspaper for easier later removal and sanded them down to the required size. These were then removed and one of each glued over the spokes. When set I carefully removed the whole from the paper, turned it over and glued the other rim and hub in place. As *Crocodile* has two wheels, I repeated the process. A drum or barrel for the tiller rope was next turned and the hole for the shaft drilled.

To find the centre of the wheel I turned up an extra section the same diameter as the wheel and drilled a hole dead centre. By placing this over the finished wheel and lining it up I was able to locate the wheel's centre. A shaft of brass wire was used and two small caps turned and fitted over the ends of the shaft. I found the boxwood and apple blended in very well when given a coat or two of shellac.

In this ship the wheel was positioned immediately ahead of the mizzenmast, which appears to be the

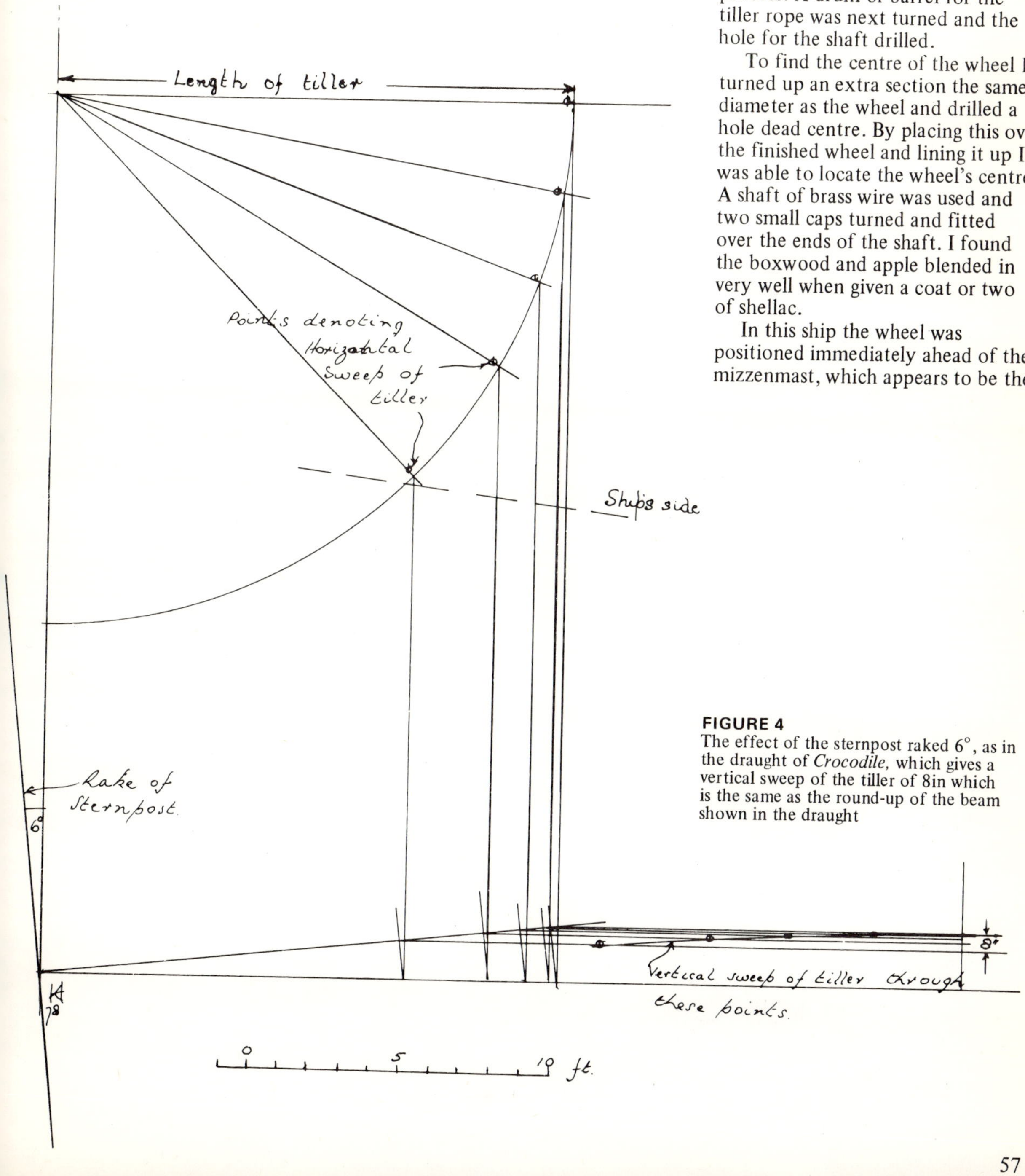

FIGURE 4
The effect of the sternpost raked 6°, as in the draught of *Crocodile,* which gives a vertical sweep of the tiller of 8in which is the same as the round-up of the beam shown in the draught

English practice. Draughts of some vessels of this period (late eighteenth century) show the wheel abaft the mizzen. In fact, many of Chapman's plates in his well known *Architectura Navalis* show this arrangement. Generally, too, his sternposts rake more than others I have studied. One plate (XXXVI) shows a frigate with the sweep about two-thirds the way along the tiller with the tiller ropes led directly to the ship's side quite separately.

The whole exercise of constructing the wheel was enjoyable and produced a satisfying result.

ACKNOWLEDGEMENT

I am indebted to John H Hardland for describing the evolution of the steering wheel some years ago in *The Mariner's Mirror* of February 1972.

KEY TO SKETCH OF STEERING ARRANGEMENT

1 Barrel or drum
2 Wheel. Ship's head will turn same way as wheel
3 Coamings, port and starboard, for tiller ropes
4 Aperture for mizzenmast
5 Tiller ropes – according to Falconer, five turns of untarred hemp secured in centre to show when rudder is amidships. Midship spoke had Turk's head or brass cap
6 Gun deck beam
7 Gooseneck supporting tiller on quadrant
8 Tensioning tackle
9 Tiller
10 Rudder aperture
11 Stern timber
12 Lower counter planking
13 Pintle and gudgeon on rudder and sternpost respectively
14 Wing transom
15 Rudder
16 Bearding of rudder
17 Sternpost
18 Sternpost knee or standard
19 Section through sweep showing sheave and iron plate to take wear of gooseneck. Several sheaves were evenly spaced along sweep
20 Lead block attached to ship's side
21 Tiller sweep or quadrant
22 Lignum vitae sheaves port and starboard
23 Spectacle plate with tiller ropes rove through to tensioning tackle

FIGURE 5
Steering arrangement for an eighteenth century Sixth Rate

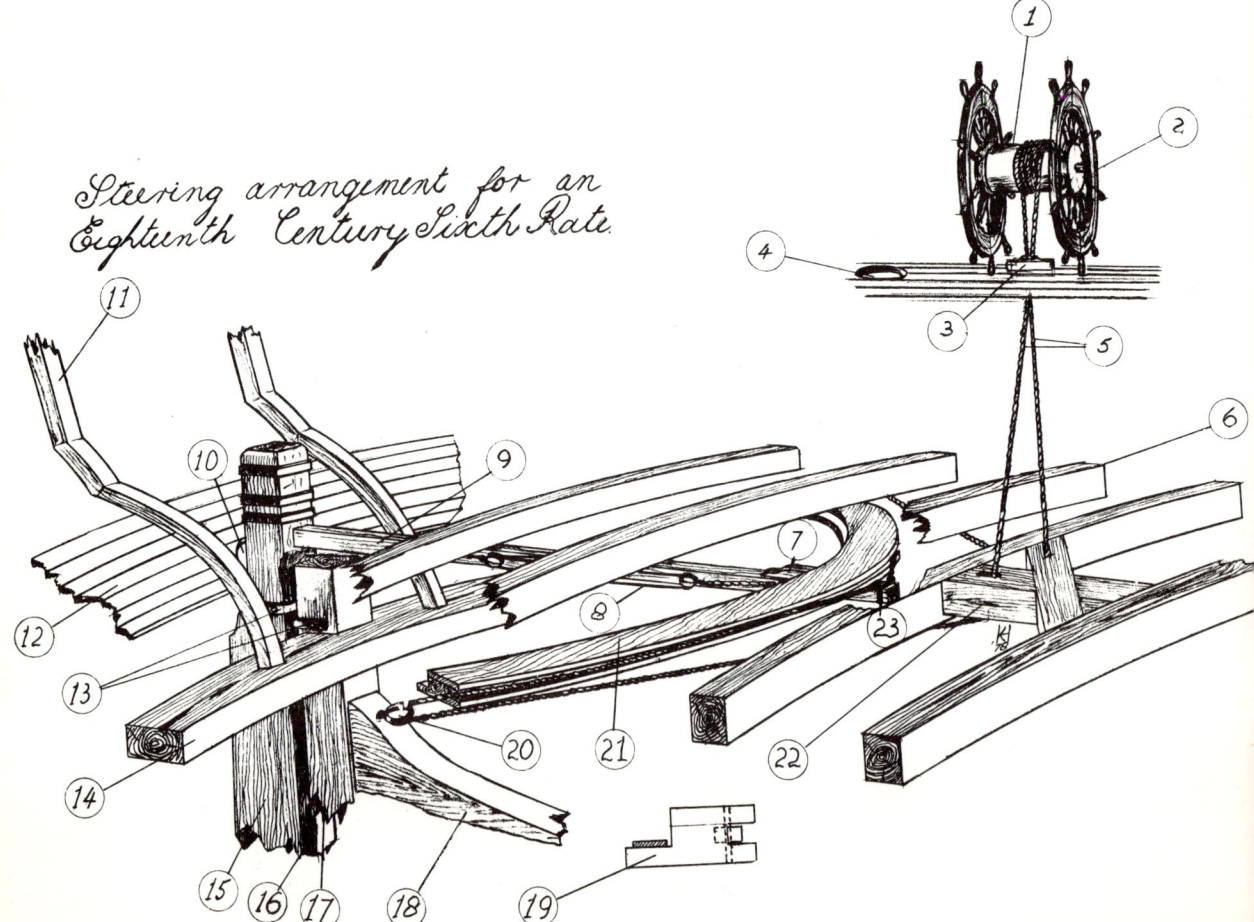

Steering arrangement for an Eighteenth Century Sixth Rate.

SITTAN
~AN ALTERNATIVE VIEW

by Ray Cattle

Below: *Sittan* under way; note the air of realism imparted by the inclusion of the man at the wheel. *(Photo: R Vine)*

Imagine a vessel fast approaching its last voyage, her name already a scrapyard project number, her fate ignominiously sealed. Rust-riddled, dented, dirty and worn out, *Sittan* pollutes her way across the water to the sounds of rude comments and genteel barracking; indeed, a good slice of the enjoyment to be found in operating the model comes from listening to the 'compliments'.

Fed up with the sight of fleets of brand new work-a-day boats that people will insist on building, *Sittan* expresses, perhaps indelicately, my desire to be different. Don't get me wrong; it's not really a two-fingered salute (would I do that?) to the establishment, just a minor rebellion. Scale modelling's sacred cow needs a kick now and again and why not, when you think about it, produce something that looks as if it should belong on the pond rather than in a glass case. One expects to see a pristine finish when the model is built to sit on a shelf; it is perhaps after all an imitation of the builder's model and should be viewed as such. But when built to be operated and displayed in the natural element surely some concession ought to be made to realism.

In this vein, a 'built to run' model should have a crew, especially at 1/48 scale or greater; it really is putting too much reliance on the automatic pilot to navigate a regatta course with no one at the wheel. Hence a small contingent of *Sittan's* view can be seen, enough to create an atmosphere but no more. A few well-placed figures can do wonders for a model; on the other hand, over-indulgence can ruin it. I once saw an otherwise excellent static model which sadly resembled an ant heap, with every possible member of its not inconsiderable crew performing some evolution or other (though to be fair some restraint must have been exercised – I couldn't find the ship's cat anywhere!)

The hull owes its construction to a composite of GRP, ply and aluminium, the surface fully plated out in gum paper and each plate 'riveted' with hypodermically dispensed white glue. Rightly, I suppose, it is very difficult to obtain hypodermic needles and syringes by normal means (I am sure chemists don't believe in modellers – they probably think we main line Cascamite!) Luckily for me, a more direct source of supply presented itself. The needles come in sterilised plastic tubes, and being by nature an unrepentant hoarder these were

Below: the anchor windlass and entrance (companionway) to the fore cabin.
Bottom: the bridge, showing the steering gypsy and telegraph; note the port navigation light.
Opposite top: note the meat safe, seen to the right of the ladder, and the detail of the cowl ventilator.
Centre: the engine casing with cowl ventilators and row of fire buckets.
Bottom: the after end of the tug, showing tow bars, towing hawser, and old tyre fenders.
(All uncredited photographs by the author).

carefully put away until a use could be found. Eventually *Sittan's* fire buckets, lower portion of boiler room cowl vents and mast lamp bodies were formed from this packaging, which could be said to be a sop to my conscience, the more so when I view the steadily mounting pile of 'useful' bric-a-brac. In the same way as the garden shed now needs an annex, I am soon going to need a shoe horn to gain access to the workroom.

Apart from the aforementioned needle tubes, the mast lamps were constructed by first turning a length of clear plastic rod into the complex shape of the lens; this then had one side filed flat to fit within the slot cut out of the tube. The characteristic cowl shape and lamp chimney were made by cutting down and slightly amending the head of a Phillips countersunk screw. All other parts were either brass wire or thin strip aluminium. The navigation lamps, being smaller, were turned from brass and the 'lens' painted in the prescribed manner with the exception that instead of a green tint to the starboard, the lamp boasts a blue to take account of the yellow flame of an oil-burning wick.

The model was finished, as the accompaning photographs should illustrate, somewhat unconventionally. The hull had of course been painted normally to begin with. The contrived decrepitude was introduced later by airbrushing matt black paint and distressing the finish by deliberately scraping and otherwise 'artistically' damaging it, to simulate the passage of time and the even nearer passage of countless quaysides. For the benefit of those with only black and white *Model Shipwrights,* the colours used were a dirty brown, an even filthier black, and a positively execrable red. Certain areas of the boat, through frequency of use, would be cleaner than others, eg handrails, corners of deckhouses and stair treads. A nice touch can be added by making the treads 'dirty' and cleaning the leading edge to a bright metal shine.

The deck, of course, has seen better days; my method for ageing it was straightforward and gloriously messy. First I selected a piece of thin ply, with the minimum of grain, and lightly scored it to simulate the planking etc. Then I rubbed in heavily thinned down black paint, wiped it clean and repeated the process using white paint (my handkerchief suffered somewhat that day, a fact my everloving seems unable to forget). Next I applied still more thinners and buff-dried the deck; this leaves an overall weathered look to the wood. Finally, to create the appearance of an individually planked deck it only remained to scrape the first 'plank' in one direction, ignore the second,

and scrape the third the other way, progressing across — quick and very effective.

In the neighbourhood of the winch and indeed any steam pipe containing a joint, flange or valve, leaks or puddles of condensed water will collect. This was indicated with gloss varnish, thinned down to a water-like consistency, and applied with a medium-sized brush (a number 8 is suitable) capable of holding a fair amount of the liquid, thus allowing the varnish to be administered in droplets. The best effect was obtained by allowing the deck camber to spread the thin liquid naturally; don't be tempted to help matters with the brush. To provide atmosphere, the deck was cluttered with all manner of objects, the more the merrier; let confusion reign. Oil drums, wooden barrels, rusty tools, coils of rope, chain — all appropriate scene-setters. The towing gear is, naturally, 'well used', but under all that dirt lurks ordinary white household string (has this man no shame?). A slight brown colour had been introduced by immersing the string in well watered-down wood stain and the dry twine then had many experimental 'dyes' applied until the answer was found — penetrating oil. Soaked into the string a drop at a time, it magically transformed it into *Sittan's* ill-maintained hawsers.

Indeed, *Sittan* seems to have been a test bed for quite a few odd materials. For instance, the funnel owes its diseased look to a base coat of matt black paint corrupted by the application of several brush loads of a nameless sludge. This was obtained from the mire at the bottom of the jar used to clean my brushes. Remember childhood days and the curious drab colour of well-loved Plasticine when all the shades were mixed together? Paint debris behaves in much the same way. Applied as a wash, the effect is as good as the method seems doubtful.

To the dry paintwork a few strategetic puffs of talcum powder were blown (I used my wife's Chanel No 19 mainly because it was contained in a single jet squeeze pack; french chalk would have had the same effect, though with considerably less panache). The

SOME THOUGHTS ON MARINE SALVAGE

powder has proved remarkably resistant and nicely helps the general seedy look of the vessel (which doesn't say much for it's original purpose!) The rust, incidentally, is the genuine article, as it was felt no paint whether proprietary or painstakingly mixed would do it justice. Even rust in its natural strength of colour doesn't look right, it is much too bright when put in the contex of a 1/48 scale model. Toning down with sprayed matt black paint not only corrected the colour balance but 'sealed' the rust against being washed off. An unlooked-for bonus in using genuine rust is the fact that when it becomes wet the colour changes in the manner of an oxide, something you couldn't ask a paint to do. The rust was manufactured by immersing a small piece of wire wool in tap water, leaving it to one side until a sludge formed, harvesting it and storing in a suitable container; application is the same as paint. The important thing is to exercise restraint: each dab of the brush must be carefully evaluated and the cumulative effect judged. Having said that it's obvious that damp patches will receive their quota of corrosion, but the areas where constant wear would leave bright metal should be spotlighted and only the extreme limit of mechanical travel rusted. All fittings and fixtures have to be well 'used': a

floating rust bucket would hardly have much money spent on it and maintenance would be unheard of. Accordingly, the dinghy (temporarily stowed on the tow bars when the tug has no tow) has a patched bottom, the small pile of deck cargo is covered by a tatty, stained tarpaulin, and only the best in bald tyres adorn the tug's sides as fenders. The tyres were worn down by rubbing them with sandpaper, and as they originally were intended for use with 1/32 scale slot cars a section of the circumference was removed to rescale to 1/48. Sadly supplies of these thin-walled tyres are becoming almost impossible to obtain due to trend changes in the toy market.

Motive power comes from two Monoperm electric motors served by five 1.2amp rechargeable ni-cads. Two channel radio is fitted, one servo to provide rudder movement the other to operate a cheap but effective 'wiper board' speed controller. The switch for the radio has been heavily disguised as a companionway which is slid to one side to operate. The radio aerial is also concealed, its identity being the steam vent pipe attached to the funnel. A recent addition (since the photographs were taken) has been a device to produce smoke. This I installed midway down the funnel and positioned its switch beneath a coil of rope. At the time of writing I

have only bench tested the unit; still, it looks hopeful and if it doesn't burn the boat down to the waterline should add that final touch.

The propellers are home-produced from brass, their three blades pegged and soft-soldered to the bosses. A slight fault (there, who said I didn't make any?) to the port propeller shaft causes a small loss of lubricant, which at times records the tug's passage in the best traditions of a *Torrey Canyon* and could be said to give the pond that bath tub ring of confidence (and the barrackers further scope for comment).

I know the 'realism' is perhaps a shade overdone, but I believe it to be correct that the more you reduce something in size, the greater the need for exaggeration. I remember listening to a programme in which the BBC's special effects people were propounding this very point, by describing their 'dirting-up' of some WWI fighter plane models. They had found that if the models were finished exactly to the condition of the genuine machines they appeared all together too well groomed. It was necessary to magnify the 'defects' as it were, to make them believable.

It has been suggested that it must take courage to risk painting your model in this fashion; perhaps initially this was true, but access to the correct tools makes any job easy. Without an airbrush to give the balance and control necessary to tone paintwork, *Sittan* would not have been possible. The only skill it seems you need is the ability to know when to stop! It's rather like writing material for *Model Shipwright*.

LONDON TO LEITH SMACK
COMET

by Trevor Manning

Below: the *Comet* under way.

The model was originally started with the intention of building a comparatively simple and 'not-to-take-too-long' working square-rigged sailing vessel for my son to have a bit of fun with but, unfortunately, I am a perfectionist and one thing led to another. By this I mean that I developed a terrific interest in what is really just a nonentity model of a sailing smack, the more so when, on browsing through my copy of *Fast Sailing Ships* by David MacGregor, I came across the part on smacks. Also some time ago there was a very good article in *Model Shipwright* by the same author.

Until the advent of railways, sea transport was in common use between London and Edinburgh both for passengers and for goods. Smacks of between 150 and 200 tons burden were employed and these vessels, despite their small size, presented many advantages over the very fatiguing passenger coaches and the slow-moving goods waggons. These smacks, which were much admired in their time, were strongly built cutter-rigged vessels with plenty of cargo space, and passenger accommodation which was then considered sufficient. Until the end of the French Wars they were each armed with a few small guns. Sailing smacks continued in use between London and Leith until about 1840 although from 1821 onwards they had to face the increasing competition of steam packets.

The model represents the smack *Comet* built in 1809, and is a replica of a contemporary model belonging to the London and Edinburgh Shipping Company. Her dimensions

Below: bread-and-butter hull under construction.
Bottom: hull completed, stem and keel in place, and bulwark timbers being fitted.
Opposite: the midship area of *Comet*, showing the wealth of detail in the deck fittings.
(All uncredited photographs by the author).

are given as: burden 157 tons, length from stem to stern 73.5ft, breadth 23ft, depth in hold 12ft. Peter Hedderwick's *Treatise on Marine Architecture* of 1830 contains plans of an almost exactly similar smack the dimensions of which were: burden 174 tons, length from stem to stern 77.4ft, length of keel for tonnage 65.2ft, breadth 23.5ft depth in hold 12.5ft.

My model is to ³⁄₈in = 1ft scale. I deviated from the more usual ¼in = 1ft to make the model easier for working when sailing. Copies of

Peter Hedderwick's plans were obtained and work commenced. The model took 2½ years to complete. There is what looks like a sailor-made model of the *Comet* in the Science Museum, London, and a chat with Joe Roome, assistant curator of the Museum at the time, revealed that a very good set of black and white photographs were obtainable.

After several visits to the Science Musuem armed with a notebook, and with special permission to take photographs of this model with the glass removed, plus the purchase of a copy of Steel's *Elements of Mast Making and Rigging* (1794 edition), I was in a very good position to get down to constructing the model. Here I would like to point out that research into any model which is intended to be built is very important, and I venture to suggest that my model turned out better than the one in the Science Museum and moreover is a working model. Another excellent example of what can be done is to be seen in John Mayger's working model of the brig *Dolphin*, also in the Science Museum, and any would-be modelmakers, experienced or otherwise, could learn a tremendous amount from it. Do what I did: spend an hour just looking at it. Photographs are obtainable, I believe.

This raises another very interesting point. In no way whatsoever am I saying that a ship model must be rushed, but when you intend starting a model try and give yourself a goal — I would estimate, say, three years for a small vessel. You could aim to have it tried and tested so as to be able to enter it in the Thames Round Pond Rally in the June three years from starting; you may even be a winner and then you can go on to enter it in the following Model Engineer Exhibition. I find it gives one an incentive to keep going.

THE HULL

The hull of the model is constructed from deal, using the bread and butter method. Much has been said on this subject, so I will not go into detail apart from saying that I used Teflon to fill the gaps in the hull, and being in and out of the water it has started to open up at the seams! I have not as yet experimented with a better

filler for working models.

The hull is spray painted with 27 coats of dark green paint on the lower half of the hull and 8 coats of black on the top half, both topped with 7 sprayed coats of matt varnish. As you can see in the photograph no frames as such are used, only 13 deck beams with carlings put in where I felt necessary; these deck beams are let in to the inside of the hull. Of course I packed as much polystyrene into the hull as possible as a safety measure. The housing for the mast was made and bulwark frames and knees put in at the bow, these being mortised all round the edge of the hull. In this way you get a nice firm, accurate housing for the bulwark frames as these are subject to a lot of stress when the planks are put on, especially round the bow. I made a cardboard template to make sure the bulwark frames were the correct height and that the scale planking would fit accurately. There is no under deck to the model. I cut

planks of lime wood for the decking and laid these following (as closely as possible) full size practice, ie no two butts adjoin and all the planks are joggled in at the bow; they are held down with glue and treenails. A tip here: draw plates are very difficult and expensive to obtain. What I did was to purchase a drill gauge and draw the wood through this until it was down to the required size, about 0.5mm. Before commencing work on the hatches, and while the deck was nice and clean, it was clear varnished and then burnt umber artist's acrylic oil colour was wiped on, mixed with black, left to dry and then burnished off with fine steel wool. This gave the effect of a dirty, used-looking deck. Then the various hatchways were cut in the deck, putting in the steps leading down the hatches were required. Also for realism I made the forward hatch doors work, and so am able to open them for exhibition purposes and close them when sailing.

The centre hatch has a part of a tarpaulin pulled back to show some cargo inside. The material for this was dyed with a mixture of black and white acrylic colours. This necessitated putting perspex over the top to stop the water getting in, but to all intents and purposes it looks like an open hatch. Do not forget, of course, to show the hatch covers lying haphazardly on the deck. I used walnut for the bulwark planking, cutting half a dozen planks at a time, laying them on their side and putting on used black typewriter ribbon, nice and thin, and then cutting through to show the caulking on the side; they were fixed on with treenails. Do not use pins on a model of anything that you intend to sand smooth at a later date — and treenails have three times the strength of a pin or a nail. After fitting the stern davits I commenced work on the seats, which I made from yew tree wood. Rather peculiar to this model I think is the fact that the centre belaying pin

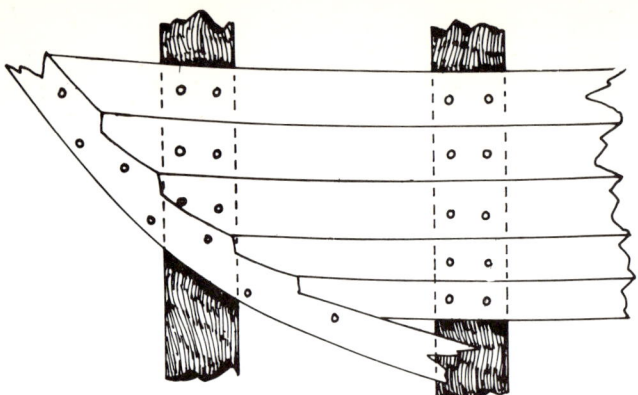

Method of joggling deck planks into waterway at bow. Planks cut from 2mm thick lime.

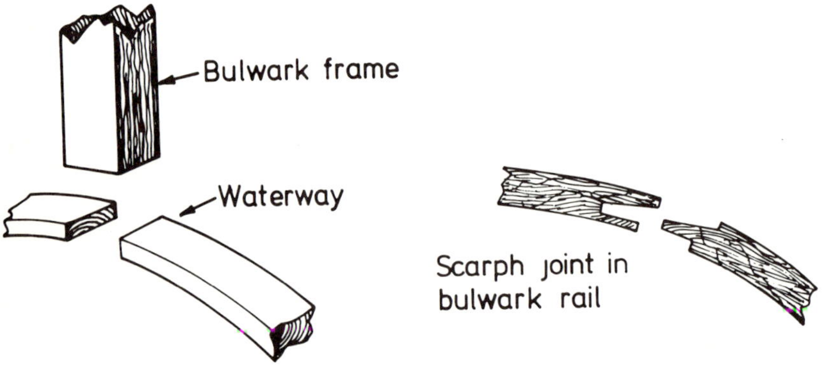

Bulwark frame

Waterway

Scarph joint in bulwark rail

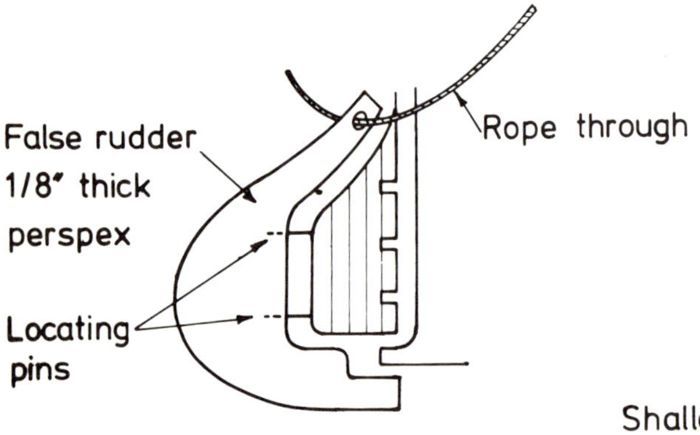

False rudder 1/8" thick perspex

Rope through

Locating pins

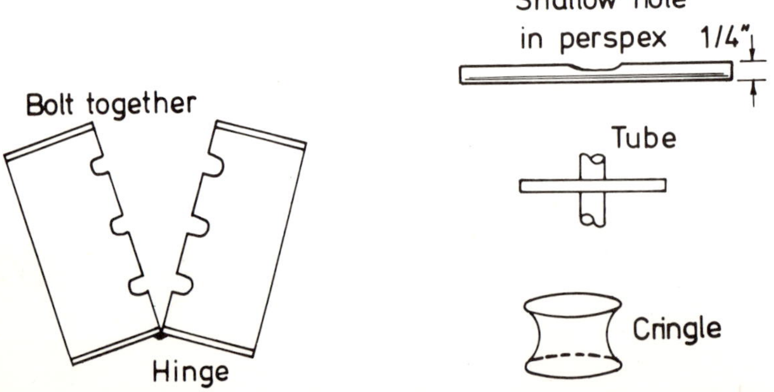

Bolt together

Hinge

Shallow hole in perspex 1/4"

Tube

Cringle

rails are an integral part of the top bulwark rail. The latter is made from lime wood and is scarf jointed just before it commences its bend at the bow for a good accurate strong fit. The bulwark nail was white on the model and was very carefully painted with five coats of thin matt white paint. The rudder was fitted, being made up of one piece of wood and planked on the outside. Realistic working pintles I have found are very difficult to make, but I have devised what I think is quite a good method of overcoming this problem. First of all I make a hard wood template to the required shape. A strip of metal is bent round the shape, taken off, and the 'eye' filled in with isopon and then carefully drilled out for the pintle (pin) to go in. The perspex false rudder that I use when sailing is fitted and is extended under the hull so there is no fear of it coming off.

After nine and a half month's work I was now ready to try the model in the water and determine the waterline, making an allowance for the top hamper. The waterline was put on using chartmaker's 1/16in white tape. The rubbing strake along the hull was made from one flat piece of lime wood, with dowel glued on top and base, sprayed a rust red colour. No sanding was necessary so it was held on with entomological pins to represent bolts.

Holes for the scuppers were drilled out. This brings me to a very interesting jig that I have, consisting of two flat pieces of 1mm thick brass, with three holes of various sizes appropriate to the scale of the model I am building, hinged at the base. The appropriate diameter brass or copper tube is first softened and cut to approximately 1/16in long; with the hinge of the jig closed the tube is inserted in the jig. The other part of the jig consists of a piece of ¼in plastic with a shallow hole in it. The brass jig, with the tube in place, is laid on top of the plastic, with the tube end over the hole, and a few taps with a hammer one side and then the other splays out the metal. Open the jig and out drops a cringle. This can then be blackened with the formula for blackening copper; be careful if you make them

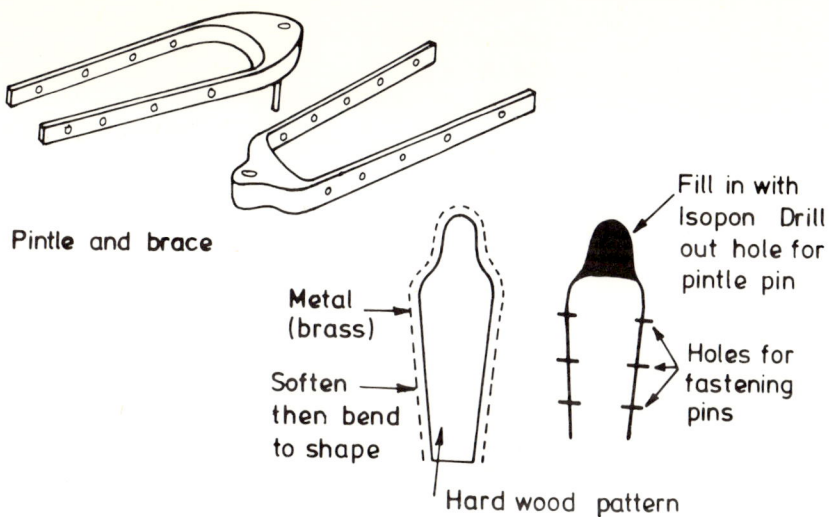

Pintle and brace

Metal (brass)

Soften then bend to shape

Hard wood pattern

Fill in with Isopon Drill out hole for pintle pin

Holes for fastening pins

of brass as this needs a different formula. For inserts into the scupper holes and anchor holes, all one needs to do is to splay out one side using the above-mentioned jig. My average time to make about 200 cringles is around ten hours, including the blackening process. As paint tends to chip off after a time, all chain used is blackened with the chemical formula and highlighted with rust, and rust highlights are also worked on to the pintles and chain plates etc.

MASTS AND YARDS
The next stage was to start fitting the masts and yards. I began with the mainmast, which I made from a piece of boat oar (I believe it to be ash) as the grain was nice and straight. The tops and cross trees I made from holly from a tree which I cut down some three years ago. The topmast I made from cherry wood that I also cut down and the gaff and boom from parana pine which I acquired. The bowsprit is walnut, is held on (the only way I can describe it) like a padlock clasp with a pin in and can be unshipped and run in. All were rounded from the square. The very top mast with the truck in that takes the flat is made from a piece of acid-blackened tube. Half way through building this model I bought a Unimat lathe and when it came to making dead-eyes, incidentally from walnut, life was made a lot easier, especially as I also made up a simple jig for

drilling out the three holes accurately. Take an ordinary hinge, drill a shallow hole to take the deadeye and three holes where required, insert the deadeye, and the three holes come in the same place every time.

Just for cosmetic purposes, the gaff jaws were made from pear wood supplied by a good friend. The mainyard was made from lancewood. I had never used this wood before but found it excellent, as good as box wood but taking glue much better. I have found a very good source of supply – off-cuts from a firm in the North of England who make bows and arrows; I will use it much more in my next model.

The save all and topsail yards I made from mahogany, once again purely for looks. The mainyard is white and was sprayed. Metal parts were blackened using the acid formula, as were all the ring bolts. Ship's boats I made according to Ewart C Freeston's book, and these took me 100 hours each. A tip: if you have to make more than one as I did, do not make them consecutively, but give yourself a break in between or you will get fed up very quickly. I used pear wood veneer for thwart knees, yew tree wood for the seats, and wood grain paper for planking the inside; the outside was planked with chartmaker's black tape on one dinghy and white on the other. Oars were dowel with metal blades painted

a wood colour. The *Comet* name was put on the side of the ship's boats with pen and Indian ink. Another acquisition from the Science Museum, London had been a plan of a smack's dinghy. Lime wood for making ship's boats and other things is, I know, very difficult to obtain. I have to get my supply from Lord Falmouth's Estate.

RIGGING
Next I had to turn my mind to the rigging. I did have a 6ft rope-making machine but found I was only making 5ft of rope – not good enough. So I made a 13ft model rope walk, based partly on Dr Longridge's one, with a motor each end, and now I can make approximately 12ft of rope in 50 seconds. In other words, in one weekend I can make enough rope to complete a model. With this model being 3/8in scale I had to spin up some carpet thread for the main stay etc, first dyeing it the correct brown Stockholm tar colour with Ronseal stain. Incidentally, all standing rigging is dark brown colour. For the running rigging I find most commercial threads are of the correct colour whether you are trying to simulate old rope or new rope. I have found that keeping a record chart is most useful. From every piece of rope I make I cut off about 2in and tape this to a board together with the details of how I made it, if I dyed it a certain colour, etc; this can be referred to at any

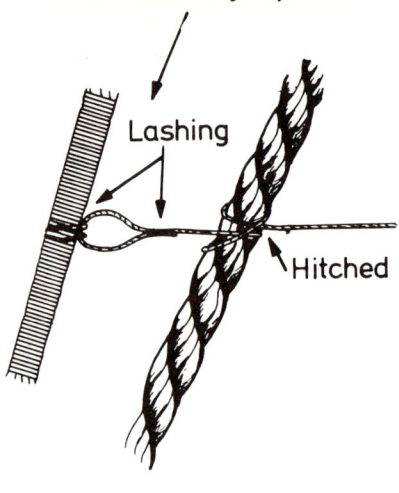

Tuck free end back in hole and glue

Forward shroud served all the way up.

Lashing

Hitched

All sails are rigged in the correct way and served where necessary

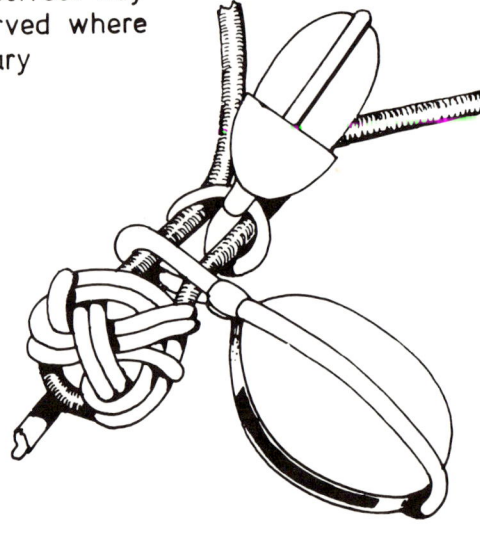

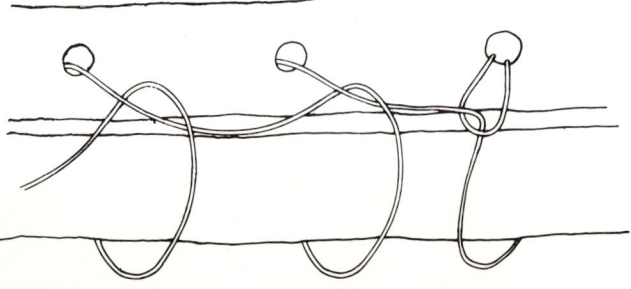

Marling on sails

future date — a great time saver.

With regard to serving the various ropes, here again I only had a hand serving machine that would serve about 8in of rope at a time. Again not good enough, especially when the forward shroud on each side is served all the way up (to stop chafing) about 15-16in. So I proportioned up the dimensions of the small serving machine to 2ft and put a Meccano gear motor in the centre with an on/off switch and reverse, and can now serve a piece of rope 2ft long in about four minutes. Here again, with regard to rope, I seal all the ends with cynalite glue. It is very clear, cannot be seen and dries very quickly.

I made the blocks in the usual way with the aid of two jigs, using either lime wood or pear wood, whatever took my fancy. Jig 1 was described by Bill Shoulder in *Model Shipwright* for cutting them to a uniform length, the other being the sanding drum also described in *Model Shipwright* — (both in Volume II No 3, ie No 7, p220). The material for the sails is architect's blue tracing linen. At the commencement of the model I washed out enough material and then gave it to my wife to wash once a week. By this process, after a year the material was nice and thin. Paper templates were first made and the material was then dyed. My personal preference was for used-looking sails and I mixed two commercial brown dyes and cold coffee together, but being careful to experiment first. This produced a nice weather-worn look. They were made on a 30-year-old hand sewing machine, and took about eight weeks to make as there were four rows of reefing on the mainsail alone each side. I glued these on as they hang down better. The leeches of the sails were served where necessary and reinforced at the the clew of the sail and down the leech. One or two other interesting points: the Charlie Noble was made from copper tube held over a flame to blacken it and then lightly burnished with fine steel wool. Bowsey blocks were used on the yards and jibs. I found that the bowsey blocks described in *Model Shipwright* were not tight enough, so I modified them after proceeding as in the article by bringing the rope round the leading part and glueing in place instead of relying on just a wall knot.

The round roof to the after hatch looks like wood because it is painted green, but it is in fact thin copper shim. With most of the deck details I do not make an item complete. On the stern hatch all the parts were made, painted, and glued together afterwards, thus producing nice sharp edges. Parrels were made from an old watch chain sprayed wood colour. There are many arguments as to what should be left off a working model, and my answer to this is 'nothing'. The detail is there because

it is an essential part. When placing a barrel on the deck I say to myself 'is this going to roll around?' If so, then it needs to be lashed down. Incidentally, the barrels were made on the lathe and simulated staves painted on with a one-stroke chisel brush. Bolt ropes were sewn on with invisible thread. Bunt line gasket, stern and dinghy lashings were made from ¼in binding tape folded over and dyed the same colour as the sails, a nice dirty brown. Dyed, grey colour canvas was used on hatches and inside boats, dyed with watered down white and grey acrylic oil colour. All varnished parts were sprayed with matt varnish. Mast hoops were made from mahogany shavings (always put in a few more than you think you need; they are easily cut off but impossible to get on once the mainmast and rigging are in piece). On the ship's mainstay there is a leather cover where it goes round the maintop. For this I took a piece of clear plastic tube from my spray gun and painted it a leather brown colour and just slid it over the stay.

I made the ratlines in the correct way with a loop each side of the shroud and a bight round the centre ones. The ship's pumps were made from holly, first drilling through the centre and then shaping up afterwards. Incidentally, they were the first things I made on my Unimat lathe and I was quite pleased with my first efforts. Handles are shown unshipped and stowed. The anchors were made with a pear wood stock, copper flukes and brass shank. All the sails were laced on in the correct manner. Sheer poles were made from bamboo.

The model works on the reverse tiller principle, which is held on by a pin and can be quickly removed for exhibition purposes.

At the Thames Shiplovers and Ship Model Society's Annual Rally at the Kensington Round Pond in June 1978 I sailed the model across the Pond in a thunderstorm! It was awarded the Model Shipwright Trophy at that rally, and was awarded a Silver Medal at the 1979 Model Engineer Exhibition.

Left: another view of the midship and fore end of Comet, showing some details of the rigging. *(Photo: John Bowen)*
Right: *Comet:* the completed model. The forecourse has been partially furled to allow the deck detail to be seen. *(Photo: John Bowen)*

PLASTIC? WHY NOT!

by Roger Chesneau

'All very nice, old man, but it's not *real* modelling, is it? I mean, it's too small and — what's that stuff you use on it? Plastic? You get that in Christmas crackers, don't you? Or perhaps it's washing-up bowls...?

All right, a caricature; but the gentleman delivering his opinions here is perhaps not too extreme an example of the attitudes we all take to something that at first glance is seen as innovatory, non-traditional, 'instant', 'not like we used to do it'. For a long time — almost since its introduction — the term 'plastic' has had unfortunate connotations. It has always had a number of popular mental associations, at least until recent years when these conceptions have been dramatically changed, mostly on account of a succession of 'oil crises'.

The first association has been one of cheapness. Plastics (there are a vast number of different types, of course) are synthetic materials and can thus be 'designed' before being manufactured to meet specific sets of requirements. Once these requirements are satisfied, the materials can then be moulded under heat and pressure to produce an indefinite number of identical articles — at great speed. This process reduces the unit cost of each article but of course imbues it with no individuality. One plastic tea tray is much like all the rest.

Mass production such as this has a number of implications. The high production rate implicit in the process is only one way in which cheapness can be achieved. Unit cost can further be reduced by

manufacturing goods to 'minimum quality', which can result in at best flimsy or at worst non-functioning products. The infamy of cheap plastic toys has done much to tarnish the reputation of plastics as workable, durable materials; and the use to which they are put in the packaging industry — hence the connotations of plastics as fragile, disposable and by analogy 'non-usable' substances — must be responsible for the certain amount of contempt in which they are held by many people.

The availability of cheap plastic goods such as kitchenware and toys has led to yet another association — that of garishness. Vermilion waste bins, royal blue toy soldiers and bright yellow flower pots advertise loud and clear the fact that no effort at simulating the original or 'traditional' appearance of such objects has been made, and, by an extension of this line of thought, the subconscious feeling is that they somehow cannot be made to look 'real' so long as plastics are the materials used.

It cannot be denied that plastics have in countless instances taken the place of traditional materials in the name of cheapness, ease of maintenance, convenience and availability; further, it is equally true that most attempts to produce goods in plastic that are indistinguishable in character from the materials they purport to represent are bound to fail (although some quite remarkable achievements have been made). No, leather will always be leather, silk silk, wood wood.

But, as modelmakers, what are

we trying to accomplish? Are we trying to recreate, in miniature, the manufacturing and building techniques that go (went) into producing a real vessel? Or are we trying to produce a scaled-down imitation — as realistic an imitation as possible — of our chosen subject, be it a non-working or a working miniature? The answer may be 'yes' to either question, depending upon the person answering it: if to the first, then the plastics advocate is in for a hard time; if to the second then there is, the writer suggests, much to be said in favour of the material.

PLASTICS MATERIALS AND THE MODELMAKER

Plastics take innumerable forms and may be composed of a wide variety of substances but, clearly, a few have distinct advantages so far as the modelmaker is concerned. Three principal forms will be met with.
Rigid and semi-rigid forms. These are the plastics which may be used to make up the structure of a model and may be available as flat sheet, extruded lengths or moulded components.
Liquid forms. These, for the modelmaker, comprise mainly solvents, which have the property of bonding together rigid and semi-rigid plastics materials by direct chemical reaction.
Two-part polymers. These consist of substances such as resins and may be used either as structural materials, for example as castings, or as adhesives, especially for the bonding of non-compatible materials where

solvents would be ineffective.

These three categories are very generalised but give a convenient subdivision of the forms plastics materials useful to the modelmaker may take.

THE ADVANTAGES OF PLASTICS

Whilst it is readily admitted that there are a large number of jobs in modelmaking for which plastics are ill-suited, it must be argued that the materials under discussion have properties which are not on offer, or at least are more difficult to exploit, with more traditional substances.

Shaping. Certain types of plastic may very easily be shaped in the usual manner — by sawing, slicing, abrasion and general sculpting — and as such may be compared to more time-honoured substances such as wood. Moreover, techniques involved in such shaping will already be developed by those familiar with other materials. However, plastics, or rather thermoplastics (which are the type with which we are concerned), may also be shaped under the influence of heat and, in certain circumstances of mere pressure, and they are able, once formed, to retain the shape taken up. These techniques will be referred to again in more detail in subsequent features.

Bonding. The chemistry of plastics allows the permanent (permanent in the modelling sense) joining together of component parts purely by the use of other chemicals (although reinforcement is often required, this reflects the shortcomings in the material itself and not in the joints) and so pinning, etc, is hardly ever required.

Decoration. The impermeability of most plastics provides them with an excellent painting surface: with the exception of clear plastic, however, *all* such materials must be painted in order to disguise their origin. Thus 'natural' substances are difficult to simulate.

Durability. Despite the fact that plastics are to the forefront in the context of disposable consumer goods, the materials we are concerned with in modelling are, provided they are treated with respect, long-lasting and immune to the atmospheric and temperature influences that might cause problems with other materials. However, as mentioned earlier, most forms — though not all — have an inherent fragility and so may not be suitable as constructional materials in models which are, for example, likely to come in for harsh treatment.

Little has been said so far about the particular kinds of plastic that might be used by the modeller or the forms in which they are available. This question will be considered next time. The writer will also take a look at the plastic kit and suggest that this much-maligned creature does have merit and is not always just the 'toy' that many modellers hold it to be.

WARSHIPS

SAILING SHIPS OF WAR 1400-1860 by Dr Frank Howard

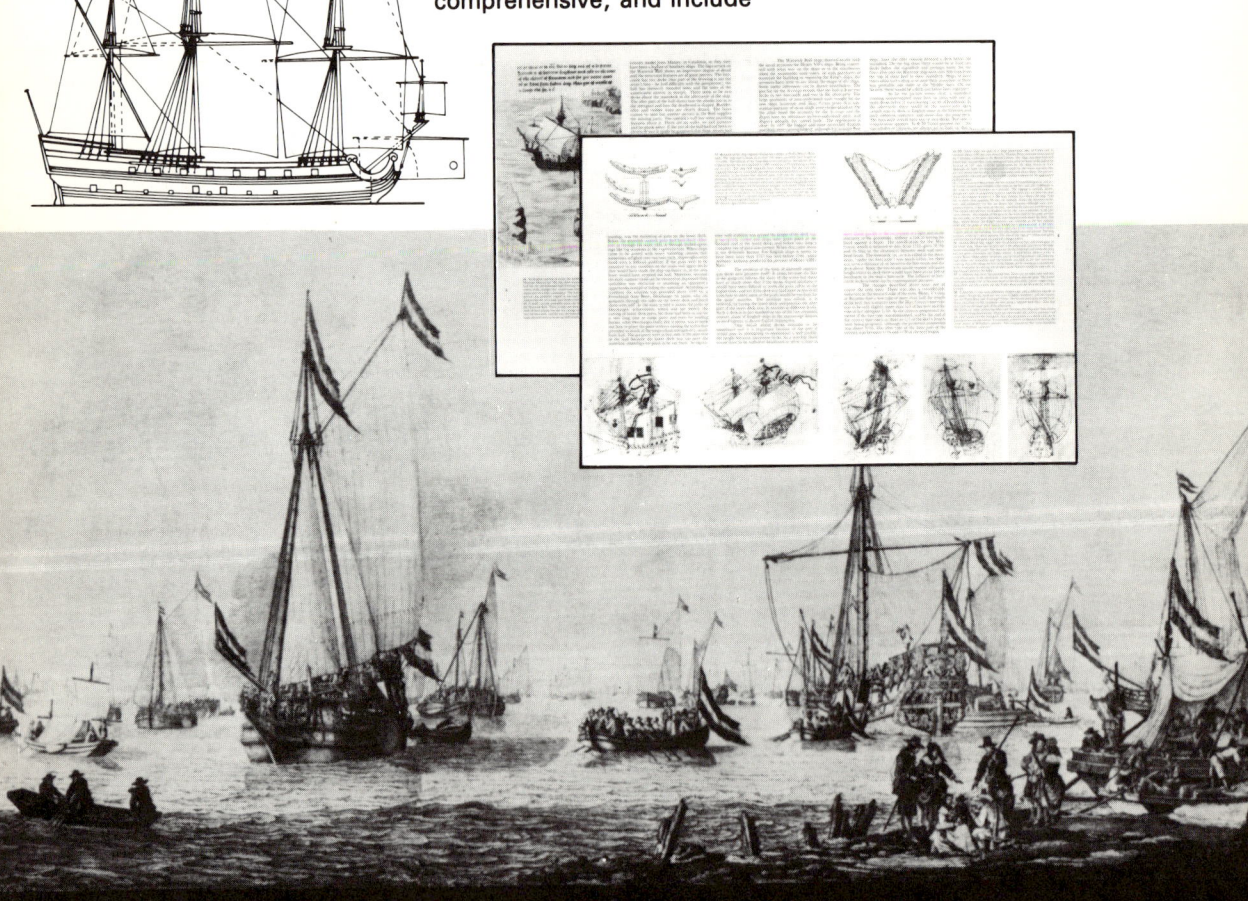

The first modern study of the wooden warship from the advent of the three-masted ship. Coverage ranges from hull design and construction to rigging, fittings, armament and the appearance and decoration of ships — in a degree of detail never before achieved. The illustrations (over 400, including 32 in full colour) are comprehensive, and include plans, models and the most accurate contemporary paintings and prints, many of which are published for the first time.
300 × 240mm, 256 pages, 150 photos, 32 colour plates, 120 line drawings. ISBN 0 85177 138 6. Available September 1979 £12.50 (plus £1 p & p when ordering direct)

Conway Maritime